2007

Men'sHealth

TOTAL FITNESS

GUIDE

RODALE

Notice

The information in this book is meant to supplement, not replace, proper exercise training. All forms of exercise pose some inherent risks. The editors and publisher advise readers to take full responsibility for their safety and know their limits. Before practicing the exercises in this book, be sure that your equipment is well-maintained, and do not take risks beyond your level of experience, aptitude, training, and fitness. The exercise and dietary programs in this book are not intended as a substitute for any exercise routine or dietary regimen that may have been prescribed by your doctor. As with all exercise and dietary programs, you should get your doctor's approval before beginning.

Mention of specific companies, organizations, or authorities in this book does not imply endorsement by the author or publisher, nor does mention of specific companies, organizations, or authorities imply that they endorse this book, its author, or the publisher.

Internet addresses and telephone numbers given in this book were accurate at the time it went to press.

Printed in the United States of America

Rodale Inc. makes every effort to use acid-free ∞, recycled paper ♻.

ISBN 13: 978–1–59486–533–6

ISBN 10: 1–59486–533–7

Book design by Sandy Freeman

2   4   6   8   10   9   7   5   3   1   hardcover

WE **INSPIRE** AND **ENABLE** PEOPLE TO IMPROVE
THEIR LIVES AND THE WORLD AROUND THEM

Contents

PART FOUR:
SPOT TRAIN

PART FIVE:
RUN FAST

PART SIX:
HAVE FUN

Introduction

At *Men's Health*, we've never settled for being average. We strive to be the best, and we know that you do, too. That's why we put this book together. It's filled with only the best fitness information to help you get into your best shape ever.

Have a few pounds—or more—to drop? If so, you're in good company. That's why we start this book off with the Lose Weight section. In it you'll learn the secrets to dropping 10 to 15 pounds in 5 short weeks with just five simple steps. Then, in "Flatten Your Belly" on page 21, you'll discover how to stay lean for life by firing up your metabolism to the finely tuned fat-burning machine it was meant to be.

Next, we put together the tools you need to get fit fast. We know you barely have time to do everything you *need* to do each day. You don't have time to waste. That's why we offer "Firm Up Fast" on page 37, the plan designed to get your body beach-ready in just 7 days. We follow that with dozens of other efficient, effective fitness tricks.

You're likely aiming to add more muscle to your physique. In the Muscle Up section, you'll learn combination exercises that will help you build strength, shed fat, and look your best. Then you'll "Pump Up Your Workout" to get the best gym workout ever.

When you look in the mirror, is there one part that really sets you off? Maybe it's your skinny legs, sloping shoulders, or bulging belly. Pick a part, and the Spot Train section will help you whip it into shape.

If running is your thing—or if you're looking to get off the couch and start running—you'll find the best tips, motivation, and more in the Run Fast section. We included this special running section for good reason: New science has linked aerobic exercise such as running not just to healthier hearts but to improved brainpower, too.

We saved the best of the best for last: advice on improving your game. First you'll learn 85 tips to keep your head, hide, and hamstrings ready for every sport. That's followed up by six surefire strategies to improve your cycling, six tour-tested tricks to better your golf game, and a seven-step plan to leave everyone in your (swimming) wake.

We at *Men's Health* are pleased to offer our best to you; here's to your best year ever!

LOSE
WEIGHT

Thinking about dropping some pounds? Try this on for size: The average amount of net worth increase in overweight men who have slimmed down is $4,085. The percentage of greater sexual desire felt by thin men than by fat ones is 240.

Yet if average Americans keep plodding along their current path and obesity rates continue to rise as they have over the past 25 years, by 2058, every American will be obese. That's right, all of us.

But you really don't want to be average, and you certainly don't want to be obese. Here's how to buck this terrible trend.

First, arm yourself with some knowledge. In the pages that follow, you'll learn 10 scientifically proven strategies to help you lose weight and feel great. But you don't have time, you say? That's why we include information on how to fit it all in. These simple strategies will help you keep it all together—when all of your commitments are trying to pull you apart. Also in this section, we offer advice on how to overhaul your favorite foods from fat-laden junk to muscle-building fuel. We'll help you make your burger better and your sandwich superior.

Here's the best weight-loss advice out there. Don't take this the wrong way, but we're hoping to see less of you in the future.

BY DAVID SCHIPPER

Lose Weight, Feel Great

10 scientifically proven strategies to help you power off the pounds

The great ones have great strategies for success—Odysseus hiding in the Trojan horse, Ali using the rope-a-dope, Bugs Bunny dressing in drag.

Your weight-loss strategy should be similarly inspired. Willpower alone won't shrink your waist; you need facts and wisdom on your side if you're going to maintain the resolve you showed in January.

Some scientists study weight loss so the rest of us can keep track of the important stuff, like spring training and Rotisserie drafts. These researchers regularly come up with good advice, the latest and greatest of which we've gathered for you. Pick a few tips, put them in your lineup, and get back in the weight-loss game.

1. Weigh Yourself Often

Time was, experts said to stay off the scale; it can be discouraging. But after studying 3,500 individuals from the National Weight Control Registry (NWCR) who've maintained 60 or more pounds of weight loss for at least a year, researchers found that 44 percent weighed themselves daily. Unhealthy obsession? No, says James Hill, PhD, NWCR cofounder and director of the Center for Human Nutrition at the University of Colorado. "They use it as an early warning system for preventing weight regain," he explains. "If your goal is to keep your weight at a certain level, you have to have feedback to see whether you're successful."

2. Turn Off the TV

Scientists at Brookhaven National Laboratory in New York recently determined that simply seeing food can trigger a physiological "feed me" response. In the study, visual food cues caused brain activity to jump by 24 percent—mostly in the orbitofrontal cortex, the area of the brain related to drive and acquisition. So a constant barrage of pizza-delivery ads on TV could test your limits. And don't get us started on the Food Network.

3. Pray the Fat Away

Christian men who report feeling greater intimacy with God through prayer are more likely to be physically active than other men, according to research from Cornell University. "Studies have shown that those who have more social support move more, and being closer to God may give men that support," says lead researcher Karen Kim, PhD. Another possible reason: "General religion in the United States encompasses theological teachings about the body as a temple, which may also lead to the consumption of a healthier diet and increased physical activity," she adds. Amen to that.

4. Beware Tastebud Betrayal

"Hunger increases healthy men's taste sensitivity to sweet and salty substances," says researcher Yuriy Zverev of the University of Malawi. This means vending machine snacks (which come in two flavors: sweet or salty—coincidence?) will taste even better when you're hungry. You could trust that you'd

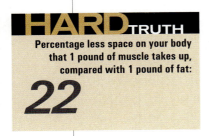
savor the flavor by eating only a small amount. (Right.) Or you could sidestep this land mine altogether. "Eat offensively," says Katherine Tallmadge, MA, RD, a spokesperson for the American Dietetic Association. "Eat regularly during the day to stave off cravings and the bingeing that can result."

5. Snack on Almonds

Seventy per day, to be exact. That's the number that people in a City of Hope National Medical Center experiment ate daily for 6 months, in conjunction with a reduced-calorie diet, to drop 18 percent of their body weight. Study author Michelle Wien, DrPH, RD, partially credits the satiety factor. "Almonds are a nutrient-dense food that provide healthful monounsaturated fat, protein, and fiber, which together contribute to feeling full," she says. Go for whole almonds in their unsalted, raw, or dry-roasted state. Fifteen to 20 will do the trick for a quick snack. Try 50 as a meal replacement.

6. Grab the Day

Long summer days can help you lose weight. "The best time to start a diet is in May because the days are very long, which makes your energy levels go up and your food cravings go down," says Judith Wurtman, PhD, a nutrition researcher at the Massachusetts Institute of Technology.

"You'll eat less and exercise more." So if you get home and it's still light, go for that run. Conversely, resolution-crazed January is the worst time to diet; the short days knock your serotonin levels out of whack, causing cravings. An Apollo Health goLite P1 lamp (www.apollolight.com) can help your body adjust to the dark days of winter.

7. Pour a Bowl of Cereal for Lunch

A study from Purdue University shows that eating cereal in place of meals helps you lose weight. Participants consumed an average of 640 fewer total daily calories and lost roughly 4 pounds during the 2-week intervention. According to study author Richard Mattes, MPH, PhD, RD, the approach teaches portion control with a convenient, easy-to-use food. Stick to filling, high-fiber cereals, like All-Bran or Fiber One, and eat them with low-fat milk.

8. Go under the Needle

When Polish researchers examined acupuncture as a diet aid, they found that people who got needled lost 10 more pounds and ticked two additional points off their BMIs (body mass index), compared with those who merely cut calories. Marie Cargill, a licensed acupuncturist in the Boston area, explains that pressure points on the body—mostly on the ear—work as a switchboard to the brain, triggering electrical pulses that suppress appetite. "The ear system is very effective for addiction treatment," she says.

9. Eat a Cow's Worth

Of dairy, that is. Reports of the benefits just keep coming. Recently, a University of Tennessee study found that people who ate 1,200 milligrams each day of calcium from dairy lost an average of 24 pounds, or 11 percent of their total body weight. "When you don't have enough calcium in your diet, you're more efficient at making fat and less efficient at breaking down fat, causing a bigger, fatter fat cell," says lead researcher Michael Zemel, PhD. Get the just-right amount by taking in two 8-ounce glasses of low-fat milk (699 milligrams of calcium), a cup of low-fat yogurt (338 milligrams), and an ounce and a half of cheese (287 milligrams).

10. Gamble on Yourself

Take a cue from the poker craze and wager against a buddy to see who can shed the most pounds. "Men do really well when they make weight loss a competitive game," says New York City nutritionist Joy Bauer, MS, RD, author of *Cooking with Joy*. "Have a 6-month and a 1-year check-in—none of that 2-week garbage." Or try it in teams, as on NBC's *The Biggest Loser*, and you'll double the incentive. You'll want to win the bet and avoid letting down your team. "Healthy competition can bring out the absolute best in people," says the show's red-team trainer, Jillian Michaels, owner of SkySport and Spa in Beverly Hills. She recommends that the team take on a swimming relay or 5-K run. "That way, it's not a scenario like 'Who can lift the most?'" she says. "Losing weight is ultimately about better health. For $100, somebody might do a pulldown that's way too heavy and end up tearing a rotator cuff." It'd be a shame if, after you'd lost all that weight, you still couldn't button your pants.

BY SCOTT QUILL AND KATE DAILEY

Fit It All In

30 simple strategies for holding
it all together when everybody
wants a piece of you

Jeff Alexander is spreading himself thin, and he's starting to feel fat.

Just 2 years ago, the 43-year-old entrepreneur sold off the high-tech security company he founded and decided to become "an employee," as he puts it. Today he's CEO at a major international corporation whose chairman has the same last name as the company's founder. "It's one of those situations where I'm managing not only a business but a family, as well," Alexander says. He estimates that he flew about 150,000 miles last year, primarily to Asia, where he's been trying to jump-start a division of the company that has struggled since its inception. "My ass is beginning to take the shape of an airline seat," he complains. "Meanwhile, my innards are turning into a cocktail of sake and tempura."

When Alexander thinks about it—when he has time, that is, between nearly constant jet lag and an endless phantasmagoria of business dinners, lunches, and meetings over coffee—he actually gets mad. "I feel like I'm holding everything together on the business end, but my body is falling apart. I can't control what I eat. I can't find time to work out. And what free time I do have is dedicated to playing with my 2-year-old or stealing away for a catnap." The strain is beginning to show, especially around Alexander's waistband. "Nothing's worse than getting the perfect Italian suit and having to stick it in the back of the closet after 6 months because it doesn't fit anymore," he laments.

Alexander's dilemma is a classic catch-22. The higher a man rises in the corporate food chain, the harder it is for him to manage his food supply. Success today means flying all over the globe, making deals over lunches at the Steak and Gristle, working the rubber-chicken circuit. A promotion can be like reverse liposuction—padding your bottom while you're busy padding the bottom line. The reward? All that hard work goes for nothing if you can't turn it around and cash it in for the next rung on the ladder.

But the statistics are as easy to read as a P&L statement: Overweight men are 3,000 times more likely than their normal-weight colleagues to be passed over for promotions. They also make an average of $4,000 less each year. And the ladder gets harder to climb the higher up you get, because you're getting loaded down with responsibilities, which makes taking care of yourself harder, which makes climbing to that next rung even more difficult.

Here we've outlined some common causes of corporate corpulence—traps any guy who's on top of his game is likely to encounter. And we've given you a bunch of strategies for shucking and jiving your way around them.

You're Tied to Your Desk

If you think racing through the day and eating on the go makes you a lean, mean machine, you're wrong. A bagel on the way to work does not a breakfast make. You need to start smart, eating as soon as you get up to activate your metabolism. "Eighty percent of the men I see take in so few calories in

lot at breakfast took in fewer overall calories than those who skipped breakfast and snacked later at night. To save time, eat twice—a quickie breakfast such as cold cereal or yogurt at home, then a second one at work. Stock your office with whole-grain bread and peanut butter. The mix of complex carbs and protein will give you energy and keep you full longer than will simple carbs, which are digested quickly and can leave you sluggish.

Snack. A late-afternoon snack will keep you from gorging at dinner. Erb suggests a cup of yogurt, an ounce of nuts, and a large piece of fruit. "It's a good mix of carbohydrates, protein, and fat," he says. The combination also supplies the nutrients you need to keep your blood pressure and cholesterol in check.

Keep the lights bright. Researchers at the University of California found that low lights increase binge eating. "Dimmer lights make you less self-aware, which loosens your inhibitions," says Joseph Kasof, PhD, the study's author.

Stay single. Eating at your desk is a lose-lose situation. Your mind is not focused completely on food or work. Break away from your desk to find some fresh fruit; if you must stay, buy single-serving sizes of packaged foods. A University of Illinois study found that larger packages lead to a 22 percent increase in calories consumed—regardless of how hungry you are. If you're so distracted that you will eat to the bottom of the bag, a smaller bag will lessen the damage.

the first half of the day that they are starving in the evening and substantially overeat," says Gene Erb, RD, head nutritionist at the Duke Executive Health Program.

SIMPLE SOLUTIONS

Eat breakfast twice. Taking in a meal early in the day makes you less likely to pig out throughout, according to a study published in *Human Nutrition and Metabolism.* The researchers found that men who ate a

You're Too Busy Traveling to Stick to Your Workout

Most hotels boast a "state-of-the-art exercise facility." In reality, it's often just a treadmill in a closet. Throw in a packed meeting schedule and jet lag and watch your entire workout program collapse. "Most men do fine at home but stop exercising when they're on the road," says Priscilla Byrd, an exercise physiologist at Duke University. "They come home and feel as if they have to start from scratch."

SIMPLE SOLUTIONS

Call the fitness concierge. Select hotels offer a service that caters to your fitness needs. For instance, they can design an exercise program for the duration of your stay or arrange for you to play racquetball with a partner they will provide. Stay at the Renaissance ClubSport in San Francisco (www.clubsports.com), Don Shula's Hotel in Miami (www.donshulahotel.com), and the Affinia Dumont in New York (www.affinia.com).

Hire a local trainer. Once you have travel reservations, go to www.nsca-lift.org and use the Trainer Locator to find a trainer in the area. (It lists trainers abroad, too.) Schedule workouts with him, "but don't go in telling him what you want to do," says Gunnar Peterson, CSCS, a celebrity trainer and the author of *G-Force: The Ultimate Guide to Your Best Body Ever.* Allowing him to plan a workout for you with the equipment at the hotel or at his gym is a chance for you to learn something new.

Try the specials. If you're traveling to Miami, try a water sport; in Colorado, ski or snowshoe; and in Vermont, hike, mountain bike, or kayak. Most hotels can prearrange these activities in accordance with your schedule. The fresh air will do you good, especially if you stumble on a new hobby. Men who participate in regular physical leisure-time activity have lower levels of inflammation, which means a lower risk of obesity and heart disease, according to the journal *Obesity Research.*

You're Always Running through Airports

Between the ride to the terminal, the rush through it, and the trip to the hotel, how can you eat healthfully? The same way you earned your promotion: by planning ahead. Big Macs and vending machine dinners are not options.

SIMPLE SOLUTIONS

Make two calls. First call the car service and then the hotel's food-service department. "Ask the car service to stock smoothies, flavored waters, milk, juice, and trail mix," says Dave Grotto, RD, a spokesman for the American Dietetic Association. Request that the driver pick up a sandwich or wrap with lean meats, veggies, and beans, plus a fruit salad, before he picks you up. Ask the hotel to make the same foods available in your room.

Carry nonperishable foods. Stock your briefcase with healthy bars like Odwalla, Organic Food Bar, or Lärabar, says Grotto. "These particular bars have no sugar added," he says. They're mostly fruit and nuts, so they'll tide you over until you can sit for a meal. But be sure to pack only one or two at a time. A study published in the *Journal of Marketing Research* showed that stockpiling snacks doubled their consumption.

Shake it up. Your sleek thermos can carry more than coffee. Fill it with a smoothie of whey protein, low-fat milk or water, and berries. Can't blend before you leave? Pack the protein powder and an Ontel Power Mixer, a battery-operated portable blender that's smaller than the thermos. Buy one at your local health food store or www.ontelproducts.com.

You're Living in the Airport

The first-class spreads in first-class lounges and the inevitable delays associated with business travel make it easy to eat out of boredom. But step out of the lounge, and you're faced with miles of fast-food joints. You can't avoid temptation, but you don't have to give in.

SIMPLE SOLUTIONS

Exercise your options. You can find a sandwich shop, such as Subway or Quiznos, in most major airports. These places give you the most freedom to watch portion sizes, and choose a wrap or tortilla over bread to reduce calories, says Grotto.

Drink for departure. "When you're flying, it's easy to get dehydrated," Grotto says. "Feelings of hunger or cravings are sometimes an indication that you're not hungry but thirsty." Drink water before boarding,

and keep the nonalcoholic beverages coming in flight (one for every hour in the air).

Write that novel. As long as your hands are occupied—while you're checking e-mail or reading a book, for instance—you won't pick at food. You know you have something that needs to be done. Do it.

Your Hard Work Gets the Boss Toasted at an Awards Banquet—Again

"People tend to treat an awards banquet like Christmas," says Steve Enselein, vice president of catering for Hyatt Hotels. "They think it's a special occasion, so they allow themselves to indulge." But while Christmas comes but once a year, awards dinners can crop up several times a month—enough to leave you looking like Santa by spring.

SIMPLE SOLUTIONS

Take two. A pair of studies published in the *Journal of Consumer Research* show that having more food options leads people to eat 43 percent more food. At a buffet, place only two items on your plate at a time, says Brian Wansink, PhD, director of the Food and Brand Lab at the University of Illinois.

Drink tomato juice. "It gives the stomach some volume, and the liquid has some bulk to it, so it offers satisfaction and takes the edge off your appetite," says Daniel Stettner, PhD, a clinical psychologist at Northpointe Health Center in Berkley, Michigan.

Ask for options. Have your assistant call ahead and ask that a low-calorie meal be prepared for you instead of the standard fare. Enselein says that healthy requests have skyrocketed in the past 5 years. Once you're at the event, ask your server about alternatives. Most caterers prepare extra fish or vegetarian meals even if they don't make that information available to the crowd. But beware: Pasta loaded with cream sauce can be just as dangerous as that glistening leg of lamb. Stick to wheat pastas topped with light oil or marinara sauce or served with grilled chicken and vegetables.

You're Constantly Schmoozing

What seems like 2 hours of harmless mingling and light drinks can often turn into an evening of puff-pastry-fueled debauchery, especially once the salesguys start making toasts. And the more you raise your glass, the more you'll dig in to the passing platters, because alcohol lowers your inhibitions for eating. Have something healthy before you go. "If you go to a cocktail party on an empty stomach, you'll eat your way through it," says Gay Riley, RD, owner of www.netnutritionist.com.

SIMPLE SOLUTIONS

Navigate the trays. Eat from the veggie tray first. Not full? Try shrimp and other seafood, then move on to grilled chicken or other lean meats. Follow this order, and you'll be full when the chips, crackers, and cheese dips come out.

Take a seat. The guy who has to walk across the room to get to the buffet table eats less than the guy guarding it does.

Fake it. To make it through a night of toasting without getting toasted, make

arrangements with the waiter beforehand to serve you Diet Coke or diet ginger ale in a scotch glass with a lime. No one will know you're not getting smashed along with the rest of the gang, says Stettner: "You're sober, you're not getting a lot of calories, and you're better able to work the crowd."

Leave your mark. Set a goal to talk to five people who can help your career or your company's profits. "Focus on the social aspect, not the eating," says Stettner. Use your mouth to charm them instead of stuffing it with crab dip.

Your Clients Like to Exercise Your Expense Account

Here's where the strategy of snacking healthfully throughout the day can really pay off. Go ahead and let the suits from

Fringe Benefits

Making time for your health pays off big time. Here are a few examples.

Retirement: Think of your time at the gym as an investment in your lifestyle 401(k). According to a study in the *Archives of Internal Medicine*, men who were overweight in middle age reported a lower quality of life after 65 (more body pain, less energy, and poorer social functioning) than did men who were at healthy weights in middle age.

Money: You stayed at the office and ate Chinese for many nights to earn that bonus. Too bad you'll likely blow it at the pharmacy. Compared with healthy-weight men, overweight men spend 37 percent more on prescription drugs (138 percent more on cardiovascular drugs in particular) and 13 percent more on primary-care visits.

Stress: A 30-minute bout of moderate- or high-intensity aerobic exercise can help reduce stress and anxiety associated with daily living, according to researchers from the University of Missouri. The feel-good effects of this half-hour session may last for as long as 90 minutes postexercise, the researchers note.

Snarkle Inc. scarf down everything that comes to the table. You'll be a model of self-discipline when the menus come around.

SIMPLE SOLUTIONS

Start with protein and fiber. High-fiber foods such as fruits and vegetables fill you up so you won't overeat when the entrées come. Likewise, protein triggers your brain to stop eating, even if you've had only light fare. A shrimp cocktail or the grilled chicken on a bed of greens can put the brakes on your appetite before it gets the best of you, says Riley.

Drink before you dine. Water makes you feel fuller so you won't eat as much, but don't wait until mealtime. "Fluids dilute digestive enzymes and can slow digestion and efficient absorption of vital nutrients," Riley says. "To get optimal nutrition [protein, carbs, fats, vitamins, and minerals] from the foods you eat, drink your fluids 30 minutes before and 30 minutes after your meals. The right balance of nutrients and healthy digestion are the keys to efficient energy metabolism." To curb your appetite before the big meal, guzzle at least 1 or 2 cups of water 30 minutes before dining out, she says.

Go wild. Wild game animals live off natural sources of vegetation and move around more than do domestic animals, which are fed grains and hormones that encourage rapid fat-weight gain. That means wild game gives you all the nutritious, muscle-building protein without all the fat and chemicals. Cornish game hen, venison, and ostrich are best, says Riley.

Look for loin. "Beef or pork cuts with loin in their names are leanest," Riley says. So order the tenderloin or sirloin and pass on the prime rib. Skip duck and lamb, too.

Your Work Trumps Working Out Every Time

Workouts typically lose priority when your schedule is crammed to the hilt. They shouldn't. By now you should have realized that when it comes to career advancement, a good workout is just as important as your 3:00 p.m. conference call and should be scheduled as such. Still, there's no rule that says workouts must last 30 minutes or require a gym. In fact, a recent study from the University of Missouri showed that three high-intensity, 10-minute workouts a day destroyed twice as much artery-clogging fat as a single 30-minute session did.

SIMPLE SOLUTIONS

Use your body weight. It's your most valuable workout tool—in your office, hotel room, or home. Try Peterson's routine: Aim for 15 to 25 reps of each exercise and minimize the time between moves. Do squats, pushups, crunches, curls, and shoulder presses, one after another. For the curls and presses, use objects in your office or your carry-on bag in the hotel room for resistance. For the pushups, try different types. In the first set, elevate your feet on a chair. In the second, place a few stacked towels under one hand and place your other hand on the floor. Repeat on the other side.

Use a resistance band. Modify the workout above with a JC All-Purpose Exercise Band (www.performbetter.com). The loop in the middle of the band attaches to a doorknob, and its canvas strap wedges in a door—so it won't snap back at you. After the squats, do a set of lat pulldowns (with the strap wedged on top of the door), then curls (with the band under your feet), then pushups or dips (with your hands on a chair).

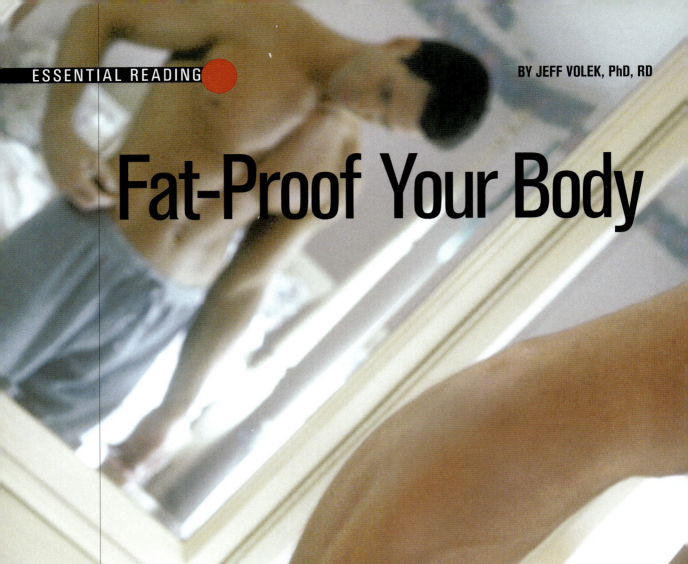

BY JEFF VOLEK, PhD, RD

Fat-Proof Your Body

Defend your
gut against
sugar—without
giving up the
foods you love

According to its publicist, sugar is a health food. After all, it contains zero fat, provides instant energy, and makes almost any food taste better. But these attributes are all trumped by a physiological fact: Sugar makes you fat. That may seem like a given, but by understanding why, you can minimize sugar's harmful effects and create a leaner, healthier body.

Eating sugar is like flipping a switch that tells your body to store fat. And sugar is everywhere—not just in soda, candy, and desserts. It's disguised in refined carbohydrates like bread, rice, and pasta, and even in beer and milk. Your body can't tell the difference; it quickly digests and absorbs all these sugars into your bloodstream as glucose.

This means most men eat the equivalent of a high-sugar diet—even if they've sworn off sweets. Case in point: During digestion, one slice of white bread is converted into the same amount of glucose as 4 tablespoons of sugar.

Here's what happens: Every time you eat sugar, your blood-glucose level rises quickly. In turn, this stimulates the release of insulin, a powerful hormone that signals your body to store fat. There's also a dose response: The more sugar you down at any one time— resulting in a greater rise in blood glucose and, consequently, in insulin—the longer you stay in fat-storage mode.

Of course, you may not be ready to give up sandwiches, fried rice, and spaghetti. But use the cutting-edge strategies that follow and you can slow the rate at which sugar is absorbed into your bloodstream. The payoff: You'll diminish the impact any food has on

your glucose levels—and on your body's ability to burn fat. Consider it nutritional damage control. And the benefits extend beyond the physiology of fat metabolism. Research shows that keeping blood-glucose levels in check decreases appetite and reduces the risk of diabetes, heart disease, and cancer. Fortunately, that's not just industry marketing hype; it's a scientific reality.

Skip the granola bar. Ohio State University scientists recently studied the effects of three popular energy bars containing varying amounts of carbohydrates—low, moderate, and high— on blood glucose in 20 people. Compared with the effects of white bread, blood-glucose levels were 71 percent lower after an Atkins Advantage Bar, 50 percent lower after a Balance Bar, and just 4 percent lower after a PowerBar. If you want a convenient snack, avoid most breakfast cereal, and "performance" bars; they're full of sugar. Instead, choose a product like Atkins Advantage, which contains just 21 grams of carbohydrates.

Douse your salad with vinaigrette. In a 2005 study, Swedish researchers observed that when people consumed 2 tablespoons of vinegar with three slices of white bread, their blood glucose was 23 percent lower than when they ate white bread only; they also felt more full. Credit acetic acid, a primary component of vinegar, dressings, and pickled products. The advice: Order extra pickles on

HARD TRUTH

Number of times more likely an obese man is to die in a car crash than a lean guy:

2.5

sandwiches, and begin any high-carbohydrate meal with a side salad that's mixed with a vinegar-based dressing, such as balsamic vinaigrette or Italian. Or make your own vinegar-and-oil dressing by slowly whisking 2 tablespoons of olive oil into a bowl containing 2 tablespoons of red or white vinegar.

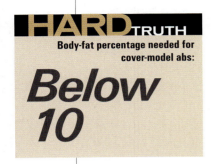

Pop a fiber pill. Researchers in Taiwan found that taking 1.2 grams of glucomannan—a soluble fiber made from the Japanese konjac root—30 minutes before eating white toast led to a 28 percent reduction in blood glucose 2 hours afterward, compared with having none of the fiber supplement. Better yet, when people took that same amount of glucomannan before each meal three times a day, they reduced LDL (bad) cholesterol by 21 percent in just 4 weeks. Look for Nature's Way glucomannan: One serving contains 2 grams of the fiber, a safe and effective amount to take 15 to 30 minutes before any meal ($15; www.vitacost.com).

Eat java-friendly foods. Canadian researchers discovered that men who downed the caffeine equivalent of 1 to 2 cups of coffee an hour before a high-sugar meal experienced 16 percent higher levels of blood glucose afterward, compared with when they consumed a caffeine-free placebo. An important point: When it's not paired with sugar, caffeine increases the rate at which your body burns fat. So, whenever possible, drink the coffee but skip the doughnut, muffin, or bagel. Opt for breakfast foods like eggs and fruit instead; they have little or no effect on blood glucose.

Add some metal to your diet. In a recent study, Swiss scientists gave men a single 400-microgram dose of chromium picolinate before a high-carbohydrate meal. Subsequently, the men's blood glucose levels were 23 percent lower than when they ate the same meal without the supplement. Try it yourself, but make sure the mineral name includes "picolinate"; the compound is the form of chromium that your body can most readily use. Our choice: GNC Chromium Picolinate 400 ($7 for 90 tablets; available at www.drugstore.com). Don't double your dose; the researchers found that 800 micrograms was no more effective than 400.

Pump iron first thing in the morning. Scientists at Syracuse University recently found that a single weight-training session reduces the effect of a high-sugar meal on blood glucose by 15 percent for more than 12 hours after a workout. The likely reason: Exercise drains your muscles' fuel reserves—stored glucose known as glycogen. To ensure that you have plenty of energy for your next workout, your body immediately shuttles any available glucose to your muscles, where it's packed away for future use—helping to reduce blood-glucose levels. So until glycogen levels are replenished, which can take several hours, high-sugar foods aren't as detrimental. Because aerobic exercise calls on glycogen, too, you can expect a similar effect from your cardio session.

Try a natural supplement. When University of Scranton researchers gave study participants 1,500 milligrams of *Phaseolus vulgaris* extract (derived from white kidney beans) before a high-sugar meal, the test subjects' blood glucose levels were 57 percent lower 2 hours later, compared with when they consumed a placebo. The mechanism? Phaseolus vulgaris inhibits the enzyme that breaks down starchy carbohydrates—any type of grain or potato—in your gut. The product tested in the study was Phase 2 Starch Blocker ($25 for 120 capsules; www.cvs.com).

The Replacements

Rumors about sugar substitutes never seem to die. Aspartame causes brain tumors in rats! Stevia is a miracle food quashed by powerful sugar lobbyists! Here, we separate fact from fiction and give you the sweet truth.

SUGAR SUBSTITUTE	WHAT IT IS	CALORIES	FLAVOR PROFILE	POSSIBLE SIDE EFFECTS
Saccharin (Sweet'N Low)	Product of a reaction between sulfur dioxide, chlorine, ammonia, and two biochemical acids; found in Crest and Colgate	⅛ calorie per teaspoon	Metallic and bitter aftertaste; 300 to 500 times sweeter than sugar	Linked to cancer in rats, but not in humans; FDA removed warning labels
Aspartame (NutraSweet and Equal)	A combination of two amino acids: aspartic acid and phenylalanine; found in Diet Coke, Diet Pepsi, and most other diet sodas	0	Distinctly chemical; 180 times sweeter than sugar	None (unless you have phenylketonuria, a rare genetic condition in which the body can't process phenylalanine)
Sucralose (Splenda)	Sugar molecules blended with chlorine; found in Arizona brand diet iced teas	0	Slightly chemical; 600 times sweeter than sugar	None
Sugar alcohols	Sugar molecules with added hydrogen; found in Hershey's low-carb chocolate bars	¾ the calories of sugar	Same sweetness as sugar but less impact on blood sugar	Bloating, gas, diarrhea
Stevia	Dried leaves of the stevia plant; not yet FDA approved for use in food products	0	Licorice-like; 150 to 400 times sweeter than sugar	Not yet known; clinical trials not yet conducted

BY MAUREEN CALLAHAN, RD

Overhaul Your Diet

Transform your favorite foods into muscle-building fuel

t's a battle royale, with cheese. In one corner of your mind, there's the satisfaction of that trim, hard body you've built. In the other, there's the hamburger—juicy, tasty, covered with a blanket of melted Cheddar. Or maybe your struggle is against nachos. Or crispy fish and chips. Or pizza. Hard to believe there ever was a time when mankind could be seduced by an apple, isn't it?

To avoid temptation, you could wire your refrigerator to deliver a shock every time you open the door. Or you could continue eating pizza, nachos, burgers—all of your favorite comfort foods—without guilt. It can be done. With a few easy tweaks, just about any food can be transformed into good stuff that satisfies your nutritional needs, your taste-buds, and even your nostalgic cravings. Make your foods this way, and you'll have our blessing to pig out.

Burger

What's so bad? Ground beef is shot through with fat, and that white-bread bun offers little but rapidly digested simple sugars.

Make it better: Start with extra-lean ground beef. If you don't overcook it, it'll taste great. Chop up some onions and thawed frozen spinach and mix them into the beef. The vegetables add vitamins and replace some of the moisture lost when you switched to leaner ground beef. Better yet, build those burgers with grass-fed beef or lean ground buffalo, at roughly 4 grams of fat per 4 ounces. Researchers at Purdue University found that wild game and grass-fed meats have higher levels of good-for-the-brain and good-for-the-heart omega-3 fatty acids. Top it all off with a whole wheat bun for some fiber.

You lose: 6 grams saturated fat

You gain: Allicin, 47 micrograms beta-carotene, 5 grams fiber

Breakfast Sausage-and-Egg Biscuit

What's so bad? The sausage patty is fatty (about 10 grams per puck), and the biscuit is nearly devoid of nutrition yet contains 8 grams of fat.

Make it better: Do this yourself. It takes 3 minutes—about the time you'd sit in the drive-thru lane. Beat an egg in a small bowl and nuke it for 1 to 2 minutes. Top it with warmed Canadian bacon—a great pre-cooked source of lean protein with only 2 grams of fat—and slide it into a whole-wheat English muffin. And have it with a glass of grapefruit juice (good luck finding that at McDonald's) instead of OJ. Drinking grape-fruit juice before a meal helps decrease insulin levels and promote weight loss, according to research from the Scripps Clinic in San Diego.

You lose: 4 grams saturated fat

You gain: 6 grams protein, 4 grams fiber, 94 milligrams vitamin C

Grilled-Cheese Sandwich

What's so bad? The 18 grams of saturated fat you take in from the butter and slabs of oily cheese. And the white bread is pointless.

Make it better: Use whole-wheat bread with part-skim mozzarella in between. Crisp it in a skillet moistened with a little olive oil. Losing the finger-licking buttery bliss is worth it. A recent study in the *Journal of the American Medical Association* found that an olive oil–rich diet can drop your chances of dying of cancer or heart disease by 23 per-cent. To protect your prostate, add a couple of lycopene-packed tomato slices. Likely to work late? Throw in a slice or two of lean ham. That will jack up the protein count, keeping your appetite in check.

You lose: 10 grams saturated fat

You gain: 11 grams protein, 5 grams fiber, 1,000 micrograms lycopene

Pizza

What's so bad? Oil-pooling pepperoni, to start. Then a huge calorie count that comes mainly from simple carbs and saturated fat.

Make it better: Opt for a thin crust (fewer refined-flour carbs), use half the cheese, and replace the pepperoni or sausage with chicken breast, a lean protein that has just 1 gram of fat per ounce. (A little barbecue sauce is okay. Great, in fact.) The chicken gives you more muscle-building protein and a ratio of protein to fat that better satisfies the appetite. Add some sliced onions and peppers to rack up a little fiber and some immunity-boosting allicin.

You lose: 10 grams saturated fat

You gain: Allicin, fiber, twice the protein

Fish and Chips

What's so bad? There's fat everywhere—the breaded and fried fish, the greasy potatoes, and the creamy coleslaw.

Make it better: You love the crunchy crispiness, right? Try pan-seared salmon; it'll crisp up real nice—for a healthy dose of cholesterol-lowering omega-3 fats and a potential brain boost. A new UCLA study on mice suggests that DHA, one of the fats found in high levels in fish like salmon, helps repair memory damage caused by Alzheimer's disease. Roasted potato wedges sprayed with a little olive oil are infinitely better than fat-soaked fried "chips." Grab a bag of finely chopped coleslaw makings at the grocery store and use either low-fat mayonnaise or, better yet, a tangy vinegar-and-oil dressing.

You lose: 8 grams saturated fat

You gain: 4 grams omega-3 fats

Nachos

What's so bad? Just 13 ordinary corn chips contain 120 calories and 6 grams of fat, and you haven't yet ladled on the electric-orange cheese product, the greasy spiced hamburger mixture, or the sour cream. Do that and you'll hoist 26 grams of saturated fat into your mouth. Add thirst-inducing pickled jalapeño pepper slices and you'll get a day's worth of sodium in this 1,129-calorie pile.

Make it better: Start with baked corn chips (less fat), add cooked pinto beans for fiber, and use reduced-fat sharp Cheddar and lean ground round. Top with cancer-fighting diced tomatoes (for lycopene) and diced fresh jalapeño pepper; it has no added salt but still delivers plenty of kick. The whole concoction is leaner, tastier, and way better for you. Go ahead, have some more.

You lose: 677 calories, 22 grams saturated fat, 2,500 milligrams sodium

You gain: 14 grams fiber, 2,300 micrograms lycopene

Flatten Your Belly

20 ways to turn your biggest excuse— I have no time—into a fat-burning weapon

BY SCOTT QUILL
AND PHILLIP RHODES

Most of us men work harder at our jobs than on our bodies—*Men's Health* editors included. Which is why, despite our image, not a single one of us walks around the office with his shirt unbuttoned while a wind machine exposes his abs. (Well, there was that one guy, but we got rid of him.)

We stay reasonably fit with weekly basketball games, some lunchtime runs or bike rides, and lifting in the company gym when we can. But we're regular guys who just as often get home too late to even think about hitting the gym. And though our cafeteria serves healthy food, we've also been known to polish off the kids' shakes and fries, because it's easier than cleaning them off the car upholstery.

Which is how we arrived at this story. We asked some of the men on staff how they reconcile work and working out. Turns out everyone had an excuse, including long work hours, longer commutes, family commitments, and 467 irresistible cable channels. Then we grilled exercise, nutrition, and weight-loss experts for their fat-melting tips. None of that hide-the-remote-so-you're-forced-to-get-up-to-change-the-channel stuff. The result: fast and easy solutions to the real-world weight-loss problems most men battle.

No Time for Exercise

The 10-minute fix: Develop a backup workout. When your gym time is unexpect-edly cut to about 10 minutes, try 100s—rack up 100 repetitions of each of three exercises by doing one move after another without rest. "Just get through each with good form," says Scott Rankin, CSCS. Rankin suggests doing as many repetitions on the lat-pulldown machine as you can (using about 70 percent of your maximum), then doing pushups until your form breaks. Next, do as many crunches as you can. Repeat the trio until you've completed 100 reps of each exercise.

The 15-minute fix: Invest in TiVo. Skipping commercials will save the average TV viewer enough time to squeeze in 15 minutes of strength training three times a week.

The 20-minute fix: Go hands-free. You know the rails on elliptical machines and treadmills? Ignore them. "Leaning on the rails removes a percentage of your weight from the workout, causing you to burn up to 30 percent fewer calories," says fitness researcher Wayne Westcott, PhD. What's more, propping yourself up means the smaller stabilizing muscles don't need to do their job of maintaining balance, which burns additional calories.

The 25-minute fix: Mix cardio with weights. "If you have under 30 minutes, the key is to keep moving," says Adam Ernster, CSCS, a Beverly Hills-based personal trainer. Try doing two resistance exercises back-to-back, followed immediately by 60 seconds of intense cardio, such as running on a treadmill that's set at a high incline, hitting a heavy bag, or jumping rope. Rest no more than 30 seconds, then do another set of resistance exercises and cardio, Ernster says. And don't forget proper form throughout the set. Here's a sample routine.

Dumbbell squat-press (12 to 15 repetitions)
Swiss-ball crunch (15 to 20 repetitions)
VersaClimber (60 seconds)
Rest 15 to 30 seconds.
Pullup (10 to 15 repetitions)
Pushup (10 to 15 repetitions)
Jump rope (60 seconds)
Repeat each exercise set three times.

The 30-minute fix: Buy a jogging stroller and put a kid in it. Congratulations—you now have an exercise device that helps burn more calories than running. Texas A&M University researchers studied a group of people running at the same intensity for 30 minutes with and without a stroller. When the group ran while pushing a stroller (which held a 25-pound weight plate), their heart rates were 10 beats per minute higher than when they ran stroller-free. "The father can remain (or become) active and at the same time spend time with his child," says John Smith, PhD, lead author of the study. Bonus: You'll score points with your wife by taking the toddler out of her hair. She'll thank you later. Go to www.joggingstroller.com.

No Time for Breakfast

Fix #1: Redecorate. "Move the fruit bowl to a handy place so you can grab a piece or two on your way out the door," says Donald Hensrud, MD, director of the Mayo Clinic Executive Health Program and editor-in-chief of *Mayo Clinic's Healthy Weight for*

Everybody. Grab an apple, pear, banana, or some other fruit you can eat while driving. Shove an orange in your briefcase; it's your antidote to the afternoon slump.

Fix #2: Relocate. No time to make a bowl of filling, high-fiber oatmeal at home? That's okay. Have your breakfast at work instead. Quaker Express oatmeal comes in its own cup and takes only a shot of water and 30 seconds in the microwave to be ready to eat, and there's no cleanup.

Fix #3: Pop a multivitamin. Open bottle; swallow pill. It takes 5 seconds, and the benefits will go a long way toward making sure your weight loss sticks. A low-calorie diet may not provide enough B vitamins, which are necessary to draw energy from food, says Tim Ziegenfuss, PhD, an exercise scientist at Pinnacle Institute of Health and Human Performance. Popping a multivitamin every day will help keep your energy levels up, ensuring that eating less doesn't sabotage your efforts to exercise more.

Too Much Coffee, Cola, Juice . . .

The fix: Solve your drinking problem. Liquid calories sneak up on most dieters. Buy a 32-ounce bottle, keep it full of water, and drink it down at least twice a day. If you feed your caffeine habit with regular infusions of 20-ounce colas, making the water

Rules for Taking Your Fitness Plan on the Road

"**W**hen a businessman leaves town, he leaves many of his reasons for moral and ethical behavior," says Marty Tuley, a Kansas-based personal trainer and the author of *Get off Your Ass: The Definitive Guide to Losing Weight, Eating Healthy, and Living Longer for Real People.* "You can eat too much, drink too much, or have too many lap dances on the road—simply because you can." We can't help if you have a stripper problem, but we can supply some road-tested weight-control strategies.

Avoid bad food ahead of time. Pack a sandwich, fruit, and nuts for the trip. They're healthy (and infinitely more palatable) alternatives to most airline snacks. Throw in some whole-grain cereal for the next morning and skip the pastry-laden continental breakfast bar. Restock for the return trip. "Buy fresh or dried fruit and trail mix," says *Men's Health* advisor David Katz, MD, MPH, director of prevention research at Yale University and author of *The Way to Eat.* "These are easy to find in every airport."

Make do—even if there's no gym. Use your body weight. Every other morning, do four sets of as many pushups as you can with 60 seconds of rest after each set, followed by four sets of as many body-weight squats as you can do (go all the way down, until the fronts of your thighs are parallel to the floor) with 60 seconds' rest between sets, Tuley says. Follow this up with a brisk 20-minute walk.

Pack wisely. There's no need to pack three T-shirts and pairs of shorts for your work-outs. Just reuse your workout clothes for a couple of days. Then, when it's time to pack, treat them like toxic waste. "Use both of the plastic laundry bags available in every hotel closet, double wrap, and stuff the bundle in a suitable corner of your garment bag," Dr. Katz says. By cutting down on clothes, you might have extra space in your luggage for a resistance band you can use in your room. We like the J.C. Travel Band from www.performbetter.com.

Manage your expense-account meals. Eat a healthy mini meal, like a bowl of soup from room service, before you go out to meet clients. Then, while your colleagues are busy letting the foie gras fall where it may, you'll be free to seal the deal and earn the rewards. "You can be more charming and effective if your mouth is not constantly full of food," says Dr. Katz.

switch will save you upward of 400 calories a day—that's 42 pounds in a year. What's more, fluid balance is crucial when you're exercising on a calorie-restricted diet, says Robert McMurray, PhD, a professor of sports nutrition at the University of North Carolina. You're burning protein along with fat, which increases your body's need for water.

Falling Back on Fast Food

Fix #1: Cook less, eat more often. You think choosing the drive-thru saves time, but with minimal planning (and some Tupperware), you can get much better food, much faster. "Put in the effort up front," Dr. Hensrud says. "It will save you time later." On Sunday, plan your meals for the week, go grocery shopping, and start cooking. Cook a week's worth of brown rice, then divide it into individual servings. Dish out the servings into five containers and grab one a day to eat with lunch. Other easy cook-ahead items:

Salmon fillets. Cook three extra, wrap them in plastic wrap, and store them in the fridge. Eat them cold or make salmon salad (one chopped fillet minus skin, a scant tablespoon of low-fat mayo or Dijonnaise, a tablespoon or two of sliced green onions, and a handful of halved grapes).

Boneless, skinless chicken breasts. Cook three extra. Chop one and add it to a salad or slice it into strips and wrap it in a whole-wheat tortilla with lettuce, tomato, onion, two slices of turkey bacon, and a smear of guacamole.

Turkey bacon. Cook 10 to 12 extra strips and add them to sandwiches or salads for extra protein, or just grab a couple of strips for a snack.

Fix #2: Buy a rotisserie chicken. Pick one up in the grocery store's deli section instead of a burger and fries from your local grease merchant. Once you peel off the skin, the chicken is a terrific low-fat source of lean protein. It can feed one man for 3 or 4 meals or a family of four for a single meal. And dismembering it will help you practice your bird-carving skills, should you be called up for duty on Thanksgiving.

That Irresistible Restaurant Menu!

Fix #1: Start with a salad. No exceptions. Skip the bacon bits and croutons (but you knew that) and ask for oil and vinegar or the house vinaigrette. You don't need to completely eliminate taste, either. "To me, a small amount of healthy fat and calories is worth it," Dr. Hensrud says. Eating nutritious, low-calorie vegetables, even if they're sprinkled with a little cheese, beats filling up on the free bread.

Fix #2: Eat the fish. Lean protein helps you feel full. Fish is an excellent source, and it may go a step further in helping you fight fat. Recently, preliminary research at the University of Navarra, Spain, found that the eicosapentaenoic acid (you don't have to pronounce it, just eat it) found in fish such

HARDTRUTH
Calories the armchair quarterback consumes during a game:
1,200

as wild salmon, mackerel, and cod can stimulate the release of leptin, a hormone that's been linked to appetite control and the regulation of fat storage.

Fix #3: Go vegetarian, sort of. Every time you order pasta, automatically ask for a side of the vegetable of the day and dump it into the pasta dish. "Vegetables are free food, dietwise," Dr. Hensrud says, "and by eating more vegetables and less pasta, you shift the calorie count around in your favor." Add some wilted spinach or other greens to spaghetti or lasagna; drop steamed squash or broccoli into that fettuccine Alfredo you couldn't resist ordering. You really should resist cream-based sauces, though. Opt for the tomato sauce for all its cancer-fighting lycopene.

An Overdose of Television

The fix: Floor it. Just lie or sit on the floor instead of the sofa. Same time, same channel, more calories burned. "When you fall into that couch, you're just gone, but when you're sitting on the floor, you keep moving a little bit," says Charles Staley, CSCS, a Phoenix-based strength coach. "You start in one position, then shift to another, then another." That kind of mini motion counts toward your total daily calorie burn, and it adds up: Last year, Mayo Clinic researchers found that fidgety people burn up to 300 extra calories per day. And when you're on the floor, you're more likely to do a few crunches or pushups.

Power Your Core

BY MIKE MEJIA, MS, CSCS

The middle of your body, your core, is the base of your athletic operations. The stronger it is, the better you perform. Serious strength requires well-conditioned abdominal and spinal structures, hip flexors, gluteals, and hamstrings. The exercises here increase the strength and stability of your core. Do two or three sets of each exercise, resting 30 to 60 seconds between sets.

Pushup-position row:
Get into pushup position with your arms straight and your hands resting on light dumbbells.

Tighten your abs as you pull one dumbbell off the floor and toward your body until your elbow is above your back. Pause, then slowly return the weight to the floor and repeat with the other arm. Do 5 or 6 repetitions with each arm.

Turkish get-up:
Lie on your back with your legs straight. Hold a dumbbell in your right hand with your arm straight above your chest.

Move your legs and left arm underneath you to push yourself up.

Keeping your elbow locked and the weight above you at all times, stand up. Still keeping your arm straight and the weight above you, reverse the steps to return to the starting position. Do a total of 4 reps on each side.

Shoulder press with Saxon side bend:
Hold a pair of light dumbbells at your shoulders. Press the weights overhead.

Keeping your knees soft and abs tight, bend at the waist to the left.

Return to the center, using your abs to straighten up. Lower the weights to your shoulders and repeat, this time bending to the right. Do 8 to 10 reps.

Single-leg woodchop:
Hold a light dumbbell with a hand-over-hand grip and your arms straightened above your left shoulder. Bend your right knee 90 degrees to lift your right foot behind you.

Balancing on your left leg, forcefully bring the dumbbell down and to your right. (Don't move it behind you.) Then bring it back to the starting position. Do 5 reps on each side.

Training Tips

Is it true that not getting a good night's sleep can mess with my diet? Will it make me hungrier?

It may. Three recent studies linked less sleep with a higher BMI (body mass index). It seems lack of sleep may affect appetite-regulating hormones. Tired, cranky, and hungry is not a good combination.

Why does going for a walk after a big meal help me feel less bogged down? Is this a good way to keep Thanksgiving calories from hitting my waistline?

It's a temporary effect: You're increasing bloodflow to the whole body when it would normally be shunted to your stomach. If you really want to stay trim, eat less or squeeze in a long workout before the turkey orgy. Studies show it'll rev your engine for hours to come.

Are sports drinks really better than water?

Plain water is fine during and after an average workout. But if you're exercising intensely for more than an hour, you need a sports drink. Beyond an hour of intense exercise, your body loses not only fluids but also electrolytes, such as sodium and potassium, and carbohydrates. "The best way to replenish all that is with a well-formulated sports drink, like Gatorade, Powerade, or All Sport," says Leslie Bonci, RD, director of sports nutrition at the University of Pittsburgh Medical Center. Bonci recommends that you consume 20 to 40 ounces of a sports drink for every hour that you exercise.

Is it better to lose weight first and then add muscle, or vice versa?

Why not do both? The same formula applies. Adopt a sound nutrition and supplement plan and train 3 to 6 days a week. You'll increase your lean body mass, which is the long-term solution to staying lean and healthy, because it causes you to burn calories more efficiently, even at rest.

Which sports drink should I pick?

Buyer, beware. Some "sports drinks" are just water in disguise, according to Leslie Bonci, RD, director of sports nutrition at the University of Pittsburgh Medical Center. Check the nutrition labels for two key nutrients: carbohydrates and sodium. A carb concentration of 14 to 15 grams

per 8 ounces will give you the energy your muscles need for exercise. Anything less will be ineffective, and anything more could cause gastrointestinal distress. Sugar-free sports drinks and flavored waters just don't have the carbohydrates. Also, check the sodium content. "Sodium in a sports beverage expedites the movement of fluid out of the stomach and into the muscles," says Bonci. Look for 100 to 150 milligrams per 8 ounces. However, if you exercise longer than 2 hours or sweat enough to leave white residue on your skin or clothes, drink a product that contains 200 milligrams, such as Endurance Gatorade.

How should I change my diet as I go through the size-building phase of my workout schedule?

Competitive bodybuilders employ a 40:40:20 carbohydrate-protein-fat ratio to lose weight, while keeping calories at or just below

their estimated needs, says Douglas Kalman, MS, RD, director of nutrition and research at Miami Research Associates. To build muscle or gain weight, Kalman suggests a more "traditional" nutrient ratio of 55:15:30. Chow four or more times a day and eat at least 200 to 500 calories more than you need.

I want to get cut, and I know muscle burns calories. Creatine helps build muscle, but it also has 300 calories per serving. Should I steer clear?

The calories come from the sugar added to many products to help speed the uptake of creatine into your muscles. Switch to pure creatine monohydrate during a weight-loss phase, says Jose Antonio, PhD, CEO of the International Society of Sports Nutrition. It's still readily absorbed, even without the added sugar.

I cut calories and lost weight—now can I eat more?

If exercise wasn't part of your weight-loss program, ditching your rice-cake diet could be an express ticket back to Chunky-town. "You may have lost some lean body mass, and increasing

your calorie intake may result in gaining what you lost—plus more," since lean muscle ups your metabolism, says Lisa Corman, RD, LD, owner of Nutrition Management Solutions in Dover, New Hampshire. However, if you trimmed calories and exercised, your body should have gained lean muscle mass while dropping fat. In this case, a higher-calorie intake may be necessary to fuel your firmer build; eating that second burger might actually be better for your belly than going without. To determine how many calories you need, see the calculator at www. menshealth.com/metabolic.

GET
FIT

It probably won't come as a shock to you that the 8-hour workday has gone the way of the horse and buggy and the typewriter. According to the Bureau of Labor Statistics, the average man works 9.2 hours each day. We're willing to bet that you work even more than that. So add that to the 7.5 hours the bureau says you probably spend sleeping and the 1 hour doing household activities—not to mention your killer commute—and you probably don't have a lot of time left over to work out. So we've dedicated this section to not just getting fit but getting fit *fast*.

Here you'll learn seven simple fixes to build bigger muscles fast. Then you'll discover the fastest way to shape up if, for example, you're headed to the beach in a week. Then we'll share some tips from NFL pros who know how to get into the best shape in the fastest time. Need another goal? We'll also show you how to get into the best shape for the bedroom—to strengthen your body and improve your performance.

So, without further ado, here's the best fitness information. Let's get moving.

BY SELENE YEAGER

Build Bigger Muscles

Seven simple fixes to accelerate your gains

Strength training today suffers from the Starbucks effect. Just as it's increasingly difficult to fight off the sprinkles and foam when you order a cup of joe, it's hard to call yourself a modern muscle-maker when you do a weight-lifting move without a few added kinks.

"It's great fun to watch guys trying to do squats while standing on stability balls," says former Olympic weight-lifting coach Harvey Newton, CSCS, of www.newton-sports.com. "But the truth is, if they just did the basics better, they'd produce the results they want without involving all the bells and whistles."

Now hold on, Harvey. Those big balls do a lot of good. On the other hand, all these half-caf mocha-latte workouts are starting to get on our nerves. Sometimes you just want to bust a move and make more muscle. So we asked exercise experts to help us pinpoint ways to make the classic moves we all do— squats, rows, bench presses, and crunches— work better. Follow their advice and see fast results . . . without the sprinkles.

Tap When You Squat

Experts agree: The squat is one of the best muscle builders in a man's portfolio because of the number of muscles the exercise engages. Experts also agree that most lifters perform it incorrectly—namely, they don't squat down far enough, nor do they place the emphasis on their glutes by anchoring with their heels. This means the glutes are never fully engaged. New York City–based trainer David Kirsch, CSCS, author of *The Ultimate New York Body Plan*,

offers this solution: Stand in front of a weight bench. Squat down until your butt touches the bench, then immediately press through your heels back to the starting position. Using the bench forces you to squat all the way down until your thighs are parallel to the floor, so the exercise will yield better results.

Give 'Em a Squeeze

As you prepare to lift, contract the muscles you're working and keep them that way throughout the move. "You won't be able to lift quite as much weight, but your muscles will be doing more work overall, so they'll grow," says Sam Iannetta, CPT, owner of Functional Fitness and Wellness Centers in Boulder, Colorado. "For instance, on the bench press, imagine you're trying to bring your hands toward each other, but don't move them at all, so your pecs are squeezed together. You won't believe the pump."

Bring the Situp Back from the Dead

"Men spend entirely too much time doing crunches, which involve only a 30-degree range of motion—way too small to build much muscle," says Patrick Hagerman, EdD, CSCS, a professor at the University of Tulsa. "If you want to build your abdominals, do a full situp. Your abs spend more time working dynamically under tension, so they'll grow bigger and stronger. Full situps also strengthen the hip flexors, which can get pretty weak if all you do is crunches." (To improve your crunches, add a stability ball. See "Crunch It Up a Notch" on page 35.)

Is there any point in continuing to ice an injury for days or weeks if it still hurts?

Icing is meant to be an immediate treatment for an injury, not a long-term approach. After 48 hours, its effectiveness diminishes significantly. But you might have swelling for a week or more, so feel free to ice while that's going on. The key is to chill the area right after the damage, for 15 to 20 minutes at a time. Before reapplying ice, make sure the skin is warm to the touch to prevent damage. And move the ice pack around instead of keeping it in one spot.

To do situps right, lie on your back with your feet flat on the floor, knees bent about 90 degrees, hands clasped lightly behind your head, and elbows out to the sides. Tuck in your chin, contract your abdominals, and roll all the way up until your chest nearly touches your knees. Then slowly roll back down.

Think Marine Training, Sir

Ditch the heavier-is-better mind-set. "Before you rush to pick up bigger, heavier plates, ask yourself, *Do I want to look like a giant Olympic powerlifter or a totally ripped Marine?*" says Iannetta. "Being able to bench 300 pounds doesn't necessarily mean you'll look good with your shirt off."

Want a guaranteed beach-ready body? Do more total work with your muscles. "Our armed forces look awesome because they're doing 150 pushups a day," Iannetta says. "Volume ultimately gives you better size and shape than going heavy."

Determine your optimum volume—the total work you do in a workout—by multiplying weight times reps times sets. For exam-ple, if you do three sets of 10 curls with a 50-pound bar, your biceps have done 1,500 pounds' worth of total work. Now suppose you do three sets of 20 curls with a 40-pound bar. That's 2,400 pounds' worth of work—a 60 percent increase in overall load.

To sculpt like Michelangelo, Iannetta recommends reaching into the 18-rep range. But keep the weight heavy enough to be challenging. Your muscles should feel fatigued (although they won't hit failure) at the end of each set.

Lose the Bench

By working while standing, you involve more muscles and burn more calories, says Douglas Lentz, CSCS, director of fitness for Summit Health, in Chambersburg, Pennsylvania. "Except for a few sessions devoted to increasing mass, our athletes do almost everything standing," he says. "It engages your core, so your total strength increases."

A classic example is the bent-over dumbbell row. Most men lean over and brace themselves on a bench, then perform the exercise with one arm. Instead, assume a wide, stable stance and bend from the hips, keeping your back flat—and don't use a bench. Perform your rows from that position. You'll work your core for stability and do a bit more midsection work. You won't be able to lift quite as much weight, but your entire body will benefit from the move.

Whittle While You Wait

Instead of sitting around working your mandible between sets, exercise another body part. "Supersetting helps you use your time better," says Lentz. And, if you do it properly, it builds more muscle. For the best results, alternate lower- and upper-body moves, such as leg presses followed by lat pulldowns. That way, each muscle group has

Crunch It Up a Notch

Because of its ability to target the entire core, the stability-ball crunch should be a staple of your workout. The exercise primarily works the rectus abdominis, or six-pack muscles, and the transverse abdominis. When performed properly, it also calls on muscles that stabilize the hips and lower back. Problem is, many men position themselves incorrectly on the ball and don't fully engage the transverse abdominis, which is a band of muscle that pulls the abdominal wall inward to protect you and helps activate other muscles. Pull your belly button in toward your spine and hold it there throughout the move so you keep the transverse abdominis contracted.

Once you've mastered the move, you can add resistance with a medicine ball held at arm's length toward the ceiling or a weight plate held behind your head. Perform three sets of eight to 12 repetitions, resting for 60 seconds between sets, once or twice a week.

1. Sit on a stability ball with your feet flat on the floor, shoulder-width apart. Walk your feet forward as you lie back on the ball. Stop when the ball is under your hips, lower back, and middle back, knees bent 90 degrees.

2. Your lower back should feel like it's curved around the ball. Keep your head in line with your upper body. Place your hands behind your ears and draw in your abs.

3. Raise your chest up and slightly forward in a crunching motion. Do not pull on your neck to initiate the crunch. You've reached the end of your range of motion when the middle of your back loses contact with the ball. Pause, then slowly return to the starting position.

time to recover between sets. Alternating upper- and lower-body exercises also keeps your heart rate revved up and stimulates your circulatory system, so you deliver more oxygen- and nutrient-rich blood to your working muscles and burn more calories.

Don't like blending upper- and lower-body workouts? Do ab work between sets. You'll be less likely to blow it off than if you save it for the end.

Pack It into 1 Week

The classic way to organize workouts, referred to by exercise scientists as linear periodization, might actually be counterproductive for you, says Lentz. In linear periodization, you alternate training phases aimed at building strength with phases focused on growth. "But what most men want out of the gym is big muscles, and that's not what linear periodization was designed for," he says.

So mix it up every time you hit the gym: Change intensity and volume. A study in the *Journal of Strength and Conditioning Research* shows that people who followed such a program for 12 weeks increased their bench strength by 29 percent and leg-press strength by 56 percent—nearly twice the gains of a control group.

Work with this kind of periodization, and your body is always adapting, says Lentz. Include one type of workout in each week's plan: for example, Monday, heavy with low reps; Wednesday, moderate weight and reps; Friday, light weight and high reps.

BY TREVOR THIEME

Firm Up Fast

Seven days stand between you and a cabana on the beach. Here's the fastest way to whittle away your middle

There's something to be said for slow and steady. It's what allowed China to build its Great Wall, Boston to complete its Big Dig, and the marathon to be invented in the first place. But when it comes to sculpting the human body, few men have the patience for it.

Unfortunately, most men don't plan far enough ahead to be slow and steady. Imagine this scenario: It's already summer, the most popular season for cashing in vacation days, according to the Travel Industry Association of America, and you've got yours earmarked for a slice of sand-and-palm-tree-covered heaven. Problem is, heaven is largely shirtless, and between an all-consuming workplace and a frenetic home life, it's easy to let your lean, fit body go all Mallo Cup around the middle. Now you're confronted by one undeniable fact: Your flight leaves in 7 days, and your belly is going to be on it.

Most guys would shrug their shoulders and decide there's nothing they can do. You're not most guys. All you need is a plan—one that cuts and burns as many calories as possible in what little time exists between now and the moment you step on that plane. That is, after all, what weight loss is all about: slashing calories. A pound of fat contains 3,500 of them; thus, to lose 1 pound, you need to create a 3,500-calorie deficit. We'll show you how to do that several times over through a program of diet and exercise strategically designed by two of the nation's top fitness gurus to fit a busy man's harried schedule. Then we'll show you how to shed an additional few pounds from your profile with a bit of hard-earned illusion and a few dieting tricks.

What does that mean for the guy staring back at you in the mirror? Picture Russell Crowe as the rotund Jack Aubrey in *Master and Commander*. Then picture his chiseled visage as former world heavyweight champion Jim Braddock in *Cinderella Man*. That's the transformation we have in store. Follow our program, and you'll lose your gut in 7 days. And the beach will seem that much sweeter.

Step 1: Stoke Your Fat Burners

For most guys, the belly is the place where fat goes first; it's where our ancestors stored extra food before they invented the doggie bag. Today, however, with the advent of a global food economy and top-of-the-food-chain status, there's little need for it, and most men attempt to fight thousands of years of natural selection through crunches and situps. Problem is, Mother Nature has guarded against that, too.

"You can't spot-reduce fat," says David Pearson, PhD, director of the Strength Research Laboratory at Ball State University in Indiana. "But the good news is that most of us have a great set of abs buried beneath, and when we lose body fat, they appear automatically."

The fitness plan that follows will help you coax them out. It's a series of short but admittedly intense strength and aerobic workouts carefully calibrated to burn the maximum number of calories while giving you the optimal amount of rest for building lean, fat-burning muscle.

The 7-Day Fitness Plan

SUNDAY	MONDAY	TUESDAY	WEDNESDAY	THURSDAY	FRIDAY	SATURDAY
A.M. 20 minutes sustained cardio	Weight circuit	A.M. Intervals	Weight circuit	A.M. 20 minutes sustained cardio	Weight circuit	A.M. Intervals
P.M. Repeat		P.M. Repeat		P.M. Repeat		P.M. Repeat

THE WEIGHT WORKOUT

When most people think of losing weight, they think of hitting the jogging path or slogging it out on a rowing machine. They're right, but only in part. Building muscle is just as important as aerobic exercise when it comes to long-term weight management—perhaps even more so. The reason is simple: A pound of muscle requires your body to burn 50 calories a day to maintain it. Add 3 pounds of new muscle, and your body will burn through an additional 1,050 calories per week just sitting around.

To build the most muscle in the least time, we've focused here on compound exercises, which engage as many muscles at once as possible. For example, a dumbbell curl exercises just one muscle group—your biceps. A dumbbell squat, on the other hand, exercises every muscle in your legs, including your quadriceps, hamstrings, calves, and glutes, and that translates into more lean tissue growth, more calories burned, and more admiring glances on the white sand.

To further accelerate your fat burn, you'll perform the workout as a circuit, a training technique that involves moving from exercise to exercise with little or no rest in between. (See "The 7-Day Fitness Plan" above.) "That will keep your heart rate elevated, giving you the same fat-burning benefit of a cardio workout without ever having to lace up your running shoes," says Myatt Murphy, author of *The Body You Want in the Time You Have.*

And here's the secret genius of this workout: You'll keep burning fat for more than a day after you hit the showers! It's called the afterburn effect, and it's yet another way that weight training helps you boil the blubber. A recent Ohio University study found that after performing a short but hard weight-training circuit of three exercises for 31 minutes, the subjects continued to burn more calories than normal for up to 38 hours.

Begin by jogging in place or jumping rope for 2 minutes to warm up, and then run through the routine on page 40 twice for a 30-minute workout. If you want to see

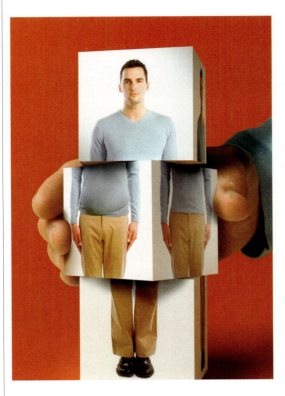

maximum results, you should feel complete muscular exhaustion after every set. "This will force your muscles to grow and adapt in preparation for the next time they encounter that stress," says Murphy. Here's what to do.

Partial dumbbell squat: Stand with a light dumbbell in each hand, arms at your sides, palms facing in. Keeping your back straight, squat down 6 to 8 inches, and then rise back up. Do 12 to 15 reps.

Wide-grip pullup: Hang from a chinup bar with your palms facing front and your hands placed slightly more than shoulder-width apart. Pull yourself up until your chest touches the bar, then lower. Do as many reps as possible.

Front-back lunge: Stand with your feet hip-width apart, your arms at your sides, and a light dumbbell in each hand. Step forward with your right foot, bending your right knee until your right thigh is parallel to the floor. Quickly push yourself up and step back with your right foot into a back lunge. Do 12 to 15 repetitions with each leg.

Pushup: Get into a classic pushup position (hands shoulder-width apart, legs extended behind you). Keeping your back straight, lower your chest to the floor, and then push up. Do as many reps as possible.

Two-arm dumbbell row: Stand with your feet shoulder-width apart and a light dumbbell in each hand. Bend forward until your torso is almost parallel to the floor and your arms are hanging straight down, palms facing in. Lift the weights until they reach the edge of your chest, pause, and then lower them. Do 12 to 15 reps.

Race-car crunch: Lie on your back with your knees bent and feet flat on the floor. Hold a light weight plate with both hands and extend your arms toward your knees. Keeping your arms extended, lift your shoulders off the floor and twist to the right so that the weight ends up to the outside of your right knee. Then twist back to the starting position. Repeat, this time twisting to the left. Alternate from side to side for as many reps as possible.

Twisting press: Hold a pair of dumbbells in front of your shoulders, palms facing in. Gently squeeze your shoulder blades together and then press the weights up, twisting your wrists out as you lift until your palms face away from you. Lower the weights to the starting position as you rotate your palms back in and spread your shoulder blades apart. Do 10 to 15 reps.

Twisting toe touch: Lie flat on your back and raise your arms and legs straight up so that your feet and hands point toward the ceiling. Holding this position, slowly curl your torso and twist to the right, touching the outside of your left hand to the outside of your right ankle. Lower and repeat, this time twisting to the left. Do as many reps as possible.

THE CARDIO WORKOUT

Each cardio workout is broken down into two short sessions—one in the morning and one in the evening. (See "The 7-Day Fitness Plan" on page 39.) We've organized it this way for two reasons: First, it's easier to push yourself a little harder during shorter workouts. Second, "aerobic exercise naturally revs your metabolism for up to an hour after you work out," says Murphy. "By doing two smaller workouts, you'll rev it twice daily, forcing your body to burn more calories for an extra hour each day."

The evening session is particularly important in that regard, according to a recent study from the University of Chicago. Researchers there found that exercising late in the day elicits the largest increase in the production of two hormones that are essential for burning fat—cortisol and thyrotropin. Start by warming up with a brisk walk or other light activity for 2 minutes. Then pick the cardio workout of your choice— jogging, biking, hitting the stairclimber,

whatever—and perform it for 20 minutes. The more you mix it up, the better.

The key, however, is to monitor your intensity level: You'll know you're where you need to be if you find it difficult (but not impossible) to carry on a conversation. That means your heart rate is around 65 to 75 percent of its maximum. This pace is considered the optimal fat-burning range, and it forces your body to use a higher percentage of stored calories—otherwise known as your fat belly—for fuel, rather than squander its limited supply of glycogen (a form of glucose that's stored in your muscles and used for quick energy).

THE INTERVAL WORKOUT

The third portion of our fitness plan focuses on interval training, a technique that entails alternating between periods of intense exercise and active rest, such as 1 minute of sprinting followed by 1 minute of walking. Our strategy is simple: to force your body to adapt and condition itself by constantly changing the workout intensity. "The result is accelerated muscle growth, reduced body fat, and higher cardiovascular fitness," says Murphy.

Like the cardio workout, the interval workout is split into two daily sessions, one in the morning and one in the evening. (See "The 7-Day Fitness Plan" on page 39.) But this time, the benefits will be more akin to those you get from weight training. That's because short bouts of intense exercise dramatically increase the afterburn effect. In a study at Laval University in Quebec, researchers

The Eating Plan

Consider this day 1 of your new eating plan, but by no means consider any part of it written in stone. Select whatever you like for each meal or snack from the options below, and your calorie count will never exceed 2,100 per day.

8 a.m. breakfast: 350 calories

Option 1: 1 cup whole grain cereal with 1 cup skim milk and ¾ cup blueberries

Option 2: 2 slices whole grain toast, ½ cup cottage cheese, ½ banana

Option 3: 2 low-fat whole-grain waffles, 1 tablespoon peanut butter, 1 orange

11 a.m. snack: 200 calories

Option 1: 1 cup nonfat yogurt with 2 table-spoons raisins

Option 2: 1 whole grain pita with 1-ounce slice low-fat cheese

Option 3: Milkshake made with 1 cup skim milk, ½ banana, and 4 ice cubes

1 p.m. lunch: 550 calories

Option 1: 2 slices whole-grain bread with lean turkey, lettuce, tomatoes, and 2 teaspoons light mayonnaise; 1 medium apple

Option 2: Mixed-green salad with an array of brightly colored vegetables (red and yellow peppers, tomatoes, leafy greens), 4 ounces grilled-chicken strips, ⅓ cup chickpeas, 2 teaspoons olive oil, and balsamic vinegar; 1 small whole grain roll; 1 medium peach

Option 3: Mixed-green salad with shredded carrots and 1 tablespoon salad dressing, 1 slice pizza, 1 pear

4 p.m. snack: 200 calories

4 whole-grain crackers with 1 tablespoon peanut butter

6 p.m. dinner: 600 calories

Option 1: 4 ounces grilled fish, 1 medium sweet potato, 1 cup spinach or deep-green vegetable, mixed-green salad with shredded carrots and 1 tablespoon salad dressing, 10 cherries

Option 2: 4 ounces grilled chicken, 1 medium sweet potato, 1 cup spinach or broccoli, mixed-green salad with shredded carrots and 1 tablespoon salad dressing, ½ pink grapefruit

Option 3: 2 (6-inch) tortillas with 4 ounces lean ground beef, sautéed mushrooms (in 1 teaspoon oil), chopped lettuce and tomatoes, and 2 tablespoons avocado; 12 grapes

8 p.m. snack: 200 calories

1 multigrain English muffin with 1-ounce slice low-fat cheese

Daily calorie total: 2,100

found that cyclists who incorporated intervals into their weekly routines burned nine times more fat by the end of the study than those who didn't, with most of that fat burning taking place after their workouts.

For each interval session, pick a high-intensity activity (jumping rope, running fast, cycling in a high gear) and exercise as hard as you can for 15 seconds; then quickly switch to a low-intensity activity (walking, cycling in a low gear) and exercise for 45 seconds. Repeat this cycle for a total of 20 minutes. You won't burn as many calories as you do on cardio days, but, as the Canadian study showed, you'll burn far more calories afterward.

Step 2: Defat Your Diet

Experts agree that the most effective weight-loss strategies include both diet and exercise. In our case, however, *diet* might not be the right word. A diet, by definition, requires deprivation, whether it be eliminating certain foods, limiting portions, or eating on a set schedule rather than when you're hungry. "And that's why diets don't work," says Howard Shapiro, MD, author of *Picture Perfect Weight Loss*. "Deprivation backfires. Once you return to 'real life,' the pounds inevitably come back."

The fact that diets don't work is borne out by statistics: An estimated two-thirds of Americans are on weight-loss diets or are watching what they eat to control their weight, yet more than 65 percent of us are overweight or obese. On our plan, you'll never feel deprived. You'll be eating just as much as you were before, but the foods will be nutrient-dense instead of calorie-dense. "It's about making the right choices," says Dr. Shapiro. "If you constantly go to the low-calorie foods, the weight will take care of itself."

On page 42 is a simple eating plan. We've included a few options for each meal and snack throughout the day. No matter what combination you use, your daily calorie count will be 500 less than the 2,618 the average American guy consumes. Stick to our plan, and by the end of the week, your "diet" will be 3,500 calories leaner and your body will be 1 or more pounds lighter—even if you don't exercise a lick.

Step 3: Cheat a Little

We explained earlier that you can't shrink your gut merely by working your abs. While that may be true in a literal sense, like a bookkeeper at Enron, we're not afraid to carve out a little wiggle room for ourselves.

See, your midsection is girded by a web of muscles that spans your hips, abdominals, back, and shoulders. "When these 'core' muscles are toned, they pull tighter, and that shrinks the size of your abdomen," says Chris Jordan, CSCS, director of corporate fitness and exercise physiology at LGE Performance Systems in Orlando. "You'll also improve your posture, which will help you sit straighter and stand taller and give you a more commanding appearance."

You won't lose weight by working only your core, but doing so will go a long way toward hiding what's there. That should buy you some time to work toward longer-term results.

Supplementing Weight Loss

Several recent studies have identified strategies for fighting weight gain when you're pressed for time. Here are four of the best.

Eat a grapefruit and a half a day. Researchers at the Scripps Clinic in San Diego found that people who ate half a grapefruit with every meal lost an average of 3.6 pounds over 12 weeks. (The placebo group lost just half a pound.) Cut one up before work and munch on a few wedges after each meal.

Drink tea. A study of 70 moderately obese people found that their body weight decreased by 4.6 percent and their waist circumference shrank by 4.5 percent when they took green-tea extract for 12 weeks. Drinking 3 cups of tea per day will also work.

Pop some B$_{12}$. Scientists at Seattle's Fred Hutchinson Cancer Research Center found that consuming 35 micrograms of B$_{12}$ per day might help dieters shed pounds by increasing their metabolism. A typical multivitamin has 18 micrograms. Make up the rest with foods like oysters (six have 15 micrograms) and bluefish (a 3-ounce fillet has 5.3 micrograms).

Control portions. It's the most effective method for losing weight, according to a meta-analysis in the journal *Obesity Research*. Eat six small meals per day instead of three large ones.

THE CORE WORKOUT

The following four exercises, done as a group, will hit all areas of your midsection. Do a full circuit of all four exercises, eight to 12 repetitions per exercise. Rest a minute, then do another circuit. The whole shebang should take you no more than 10 minutes, and you'll start to see results in just days. Do it twice a week, whenever you can fit it in, keeping these pointers in mind.

Stick to low reps. Most people hit their abs with high repetitions, believing this is the key to a faster six-pack. Resist the temptation. "Your abdominals are made of the same tissue as your biceps, triceps, chest, and every other muscle group," says Jordan. "So the same rules apply. Stick to eight to 12 repetitions, and when that becomes easy, increase the intensity."

Go slow. The easiest way to up the intensity is to slow the pace at which you perform the repetitions. "The slower you go, the more force and exertion the muscles are required to provide," says Jordan. Count to "two Mississippi" as you contract your abs and to four as you relax them.

Stay contracted. As you're performing each exercise, never relax your abs completely. Keeping them in a constant state of contraction is yet another way to increase the intensity and get faster results.

Here are the exercises.

Abdominal crunch: Lie on your back with your knees bent and your hands cupped behind your ears. Slowly crunch up, bringing your shoulder blades off the ground. Lower and repeat.

Leg raise: Lie on your back with your legs straight and your hands on the floor near your butt. Use your lower abdominal muscles to raise your legs toward the ceiling until they're perpendicular to the floor. Then slowly lower them back to the starting position. When your feet touch the floor, repeat.

Twisting crunch: Lie on your back with your hands cupped behind your ears and your elbows out. Cross your ankles. With your knees slightly bent, raise your legs until your thighs are perpendicular to your body. Bring your right shoulder off the floor as you cross your right elbow over to your left knee. Lower and repeat to the other side.

Superman: Lie facedown with your arms extended in front of your head. Simultaneously lift your arms, shoulders, chest, and legs off the floor as high as you can. Pause, then lower and repeat.

Maintain Your Losses

Congratulations. If you've made it this far, you've shed a few pounds, tightened your midsection, and started on the road to long-term weight management. You've done the hard part. But here's the rub: Most guys don't do the easy part, which is keeping the pounds off once they're gone. We say "easy" because it requires far less effort to maintain weight loss than to affect it. The first 2 pounds, for example, required you to create a weekly calorie deficit of 7,000 calories. "To maintain a 2-pound weight loss, you have to cut out just 112 calories per week," says John Peters, cofounder of America on the Move, a national initiative to help people avoid weight gain by making small changes in their daily lives. That averages out to roughly 16 fewer calories per day.

We're not going to bore you with a plan to cut 16 calories. Instead, we'll pose a challenge: Why stop there? With a little more effort, you can lose a pound a week for as long as you like.

"Stick to the same workout routine," says Myatt Murphy, author of *The Body You Want in the Time You Have.* "Just do it a lot less often." Four days per week instead of 7, to be exact: two strength workouts, a cardio workout, and an interval workout. Even if you cut down on your workout and add another 250 calories' worth of food every day, your weekly calorie deficit will still total 3,500—enough to lose 1 pound every 7 days.

There is something to be said for slow and steady, after all. It's the best way to maintain long-term results after you've created a short-term foundation.

BY SCOTT QUILL

Go Pro

Are you ready for some strength, speed, and explosive power? Here's how the pros in the NFL prepare

Ovie Mughelli steps out of his Lincoln Navigator, and suddenly I feel—for the second time today—weaker than usual. The Ravens' 6'1", 255-pound fullback greets me with a smile and a grip that envelops my hand. He's an easy-going guy—but with threatening pecs that look like they might burst through his shirt.

Earlier, another nice guy had knocked my body image 5 yards downfield. It was my trainer for the day, Jon Crosby, CSCS, who had me do squat jumps on a Vertimax, a tool that improves lower-body power by laughing at you. The Vertimax's cables are attached at one end to a square rubber platform and at the other to a belt around your waist. As you jump, resistance from the cables yanks you back down. When you're finished, though, you feel as if you could leap like an NFL defensive back.

This is my first workout at Velocity Sports Performance, Crosby's 16,000-foot training center in Baltimore, which houses an indoor artificial-turf field, a three-lane sprinting track, and enough bumper plates to sink a navy destroyer.

Mughelli has been coming here for 3 years. He first worked with Crosby as a Wake Forest senior to prepare for the National Football League's combine—the legendary battery of physical tests used to evaluate collegiate talent.

Crosby and his team of trainers typically have 6 weeks to train players for the combine. Coaches and personnel directors look for strength, speed, power, flexibility, and agility. These players have plenty of that already. Crosby, who has put 100 players through his program in 7 years, gives them more of everything.

I wanted to see how he did it.

Mughelli, wearing black shorts and a black compression shirt that strains to contain his biceps, starts with an "active and dynamic warmup" on the track. He skips, does butt kicks, runs ladders, and does variations of the lunge while swiftly punching his knees back and forth. He mixes in sumo squats, planks, and a pack of other exercises that get him moving in every direction and pausing in stretched positions. Fifteen minutes later, he's ready to work.

"It's definitely not the same as touching your toes a few times and going at it," says Mughelli. "You don't realize the difference this will make until you do it."

After his warmup, Mughelli rips through drills and exercises he first learned in training for the combine. Just 5 minutes in, he's dripping with sweat and looking bigger and faster than before. I'd draft him.

Soon Crosby is putting me through a similar, though tamer, workout. I come out of it feeling beat but better. Anyone need a cover corner?

The following pages take you through the combine's main events and can help you build a body that excels in any sport. Have a friend time your sprints and measure your jumps. Then do the drills and exercises and retest yourself every 6 weeks. It's more fun than tracking how many workouts it takes to move up 5 pounds on the preacher curl—and more rewarding, too.

PAINkiller

Bench Press

The combine tests strength and endurance by seeing how many times a player can bench-press 225 pounds. Technique counts. If your hips rise off the bench on your second rep, for example, you'll stay at two until you fix your form.

BUILD STRENGTH

Lift as if someone is inspecting every repetition. "We're trying to save energy by how we line up on the bench," says Crosby. Using correct form eliminates unnecessary movement, allowing you to lift more weight more times.

Pay attention to your feet. Place them flat on the floor at the sides of the bench, with your knees bent at a slightly acute angle, just less than 90 degrees. Your feet should give you a wide base of support, says Crosby. Pull your shoulder blades back so there's a natural arch in your lower back.

Keep a tight grip. "A lot of people let the bar roll back in their fingers, but you want a straight line from the elbow through the wrist," says Crosby.

Improving your form will instantly boost

your bench, but benching alone will help you only so much. "You have to work the triceps and the stabilizers of the shoulders, because once you fatigue the pecs, these other muscles finish the exercise to some extent," says Crosby. Try dips for your triceps and stability-ball pushups to strengthen the smaller muscles of your shoulders.

IMPROVE ENDURANCE

Earlier this year, Brigham Young University offensive lineman Scott Young added endurance training to his bench-press routine, and it paid off. Young bench-pressed 225 pounds for an NFL-combine record of 43 repetitions. "If you increase your muscular endurance, you should be able to withstand more fatigue and increase your total number of reps," says Mike Gough, CSCS, Young's trainer for the combine and owner of www. procombinetraining.com.

Frequency: Work on endurance every other time you bench-press, Gough suggests. Try bench-pressing 65 percent of your one-rep max (the weight you can bench-press only once) as many times as you can. Keep the bar moving fast yet under control, Gough says. You can also try this chest routine:

Do 20 pushups, then 20 reps of a standing chest press using a resistance band. (Attach a band to a fixed object, face the opposite direction, and press the handles away from your chest. Allow the handles to move back to the sides of your chest and repeat.) Using the bands allows you to develop strength and endurance in a full range of motion, says Gough. After the standing presses, try 20 chest flies with the band while standing and then another 20 standing presses. If you're still not fatigued, perform another set of pushups.

20-Yard Shuttle

This drill improves agility and quickness. It's easiest on a football field, but you can place three sticks, cones, strips of tape, or any other markers in a row, 5 yards apart on your lawn. (See the illustration below.)

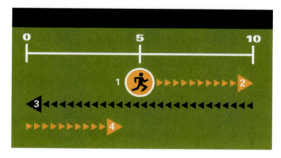

Stand at the middle line with one foot on each side of it. Squat and touch the line with your right hand. (This is the starting position.) Sprint to your right and touch the 10-yard line with your right hand. Then sprint across to the far line and touch it with your left hand. Finally, sprint across the starting line. When you start over again in the middle, reverse the motion, sprinting first to your left.

Develop Quickness

Shave seconds off your time by using a hockey stop to change direction. (Most men have trouble accelerating out of stops in this drill—and in games.) As you approach the line, drive both your feet into the ground while turning your hips 90 degrees away from the direction you've just been running

in. Keep more weight on the leg you'll push off with to run in the opposite direction.

Increase your speed by strengthening your core. The small muscles that support your hips, pelvis, abs, and back project your hips forward as you run—a key to speed. Try a variation on the drawing-in maneuver for your core. (See "Drawing-in Progression" on page 51.)

Frequency: Do the shuttle three to five times in each direction, once or twice a week.

40-Yard Dash

It's the classic football measurement, but better sprinting speed will give you an edge in most other sports, as well.

LEARN ACCELERATION

The key to acceleration is fast arms. The key to fast arms is your back muscles, Crosby says, because they help move your arms. "Move your arms from your shoulders, not your elbows," he says. Keep your arms bent and below your head as you pump. Swinging your arms overhead can actually cause you to overstride.

Start the drill like a defensive end. That's left foot in front of right, right hand on the ground, and left hand on the left side of your butt. For the first 20 yards, lean forward 45 degrees. You'll naturally move into a more upright position as you stop accelerating and continue to run at full speed.

Hit the wall. A "wall sprint" accustoms you to running at the correct angle, because your torso stays steady as you pump your legs back and forth. (See the description on

Vertical Jump and Long Jump

The combine uses a piece of equipment called a Vertec to measure your standing vertical jump. It's basically a pole with plastic strips that you swipe with your hands at the top of your jump. In your gym, chalk or wet your hands and reach up to touch the wall, making a mark. Then jump, touching the wall as high as you can. Measure the difference to get your vertical jump. For a standing long jump, mark where you start and land and measure the difference.

JUMP HIGHER AND LONGER

For better hops, add the box jump to your workout. "I want you to handle your own body weight in gravity before we start strap-ping things on you," says Crosby. You'll need a box, exercise step, or bench. (See the description on page 51.)

After doing box jumps, try three to five rebound long jumps: Jump forward and land, then immediately spring up and out into your next long jump. You can progress to doing both box jumps and rebound jumps on one foot or with the added resistance of a weighted vest. You can also try long jumps starting with your feet in a staggered stance. Doing this improves your leg power, and it will also help with your acceleration in each shuttle.

Frequency: Practice the box jump and rebound long jump once or twice a week.

BY MYATT MURPHY

Get the Body She Wants

Follow this plan to
strengthen your body and
improve your performance

Want to have great performance in the bedroom? Strengthen your core. A thrusting pelvis requires flexion and extension of your lower-back muscles and hip flexors (which are attached along your lumbar spine). The spinal erectors, which support your spine—with help from the rectus abdominis and transverse abdominis—prevent your hip flexors and lower back from tightening. Depending on the position, secondary muscles come into play to push the body up, forward, or under—or wherever. Experiment.

The Payoff

A solid base! Conditioning your shoulders, triceps, and chest will make it easier to support your body weight for longer periods of time, allowing you to hold certain positions as long as you need to—or as long as she needs you to.

Wilder positions! The more flexible you are, the more versatility you'll be able to demonstrate in bed. Our all-positions plan combines a mix of moves that will strengthen and lengthen your muscles.

The Most Important Sex Muscle

Your pubococcygeus (PC) muscle, which makes up the pelvic floor, can control the strength and angle of your erection and the intensity of an orgasm. Here's how to locate it: When you stop the flow while you're urinating, the PC muscle is the one that's contracting.

Greater power! Occasional lower-back pain, spasms, and soreness after sex are often the result of muscular imbalances. Training your smaller, sometimes neglected muscles—and keeping them limber—means you'll always be ready to go another round.

More stamina! Most men work their muscles for size and strength, but impressive sex mostly relies on having muscular stamina and rhythm. Using endurance exercises that mimic the motions involved in sex can prevent weaker muscles from quitting too soon.

Your Better-Sex Body

Building a body for amazing sex has little to do with how much weight you can lift, press, or curl. It depends on how well your body can push and thrust. "It's the smaller muscles you can't see or feel that make all the difference when it comes to great sex," says Jeff Bell, CSCS, owner of Spectrum Wellness in New York City. It doesn't take much to tap into these subtler yet sexier muscles, but you need to train them for strength, stamina, and flexibility. In this plan, Bell includes moves that both strengthen and lengthen your muscles for the three most popular sex positions. To get the best results from this routine, he recommends doing 20 minutes of cardiovascular exercise at least two or three times a week.

The Workout

Exercising to improve your sexual performance requires functional movements that train your entire body to be more flexible

The 4-Week Program

	WEEK 1	WEEK 2	WEEK 3	WEEK 4
Create your routine by . . .	Doing both moves from 2 sections	Doing both moves from 3 sections	Doing both moves from all 4 sections	Doing both moves from all 4 sections
Sets of each exercise or stretch	2	2	2	2
Your total workout should be . . .	8 sets	12 sets	16 sets	16 sets
Rest between sets:	15–30 seconds	15–30 seconds	15–30 seconds	15–30 seconds
Do this workout . . .	Twice a week	Three times a week	Twice a week	Three times a week

and resilient. The three stretches in this routine work your lower back, hip flexors, and glutes through their full range of motion. The remaining five exercises develop areas that need long-term stamina—your chest, shoulders, triceps, hamstrings, quadriceps, and abs. That's why you'll be doing each exercise to failure instead of doing a specific number of repetitions.

Begin your 4-week program by choosing two of the four sections, then work your way up to doing all four sections in one workout. In 4 weeks, you and your partner will notice a difference you'll be able to see and feel—no matter what position you try. (You can also perform each stretch individually as needed—either immediately after sex or the morning after—depending on which positions you used.)

Go to www.menshealth.com/video for video demonstrations of these exercises.

SECTION 1: ON TOP

STABILITY-BALL DECLINE PUSHUP

Works shoulders, chest, triceps, abs

Kneel with a stability ball behind you and place your hands flat on the floor, shoulder-width apart. Place your shins on the ball and get into the standard pushup position—arms straight, hands directly under your shoulders. Your back should be flat and your abs drawn in. Tuck your chin and, leading with your chest, lower your body to the floor. Push yourself back up and repeat.

Watch your form. Keep your head in line with your back and resist looking at the ball. Bending your neck in this position can strain it, and you might lose your balance.

LOWER-BACK LIE-DOWN

Stretches lower back

Lie flat on your back with your legs bent, feet flat on the floor, and arms at your sides. Draw your knees up to your chest and gently grab your legs just behind the knees. Slowly pull both knees toward your chest as far as you comfortably can, keeping your back flat on the floor at all times. Hold the stretch for 2 to 3 seconds, then slowly lower your legs. Repeat the stretch for as many repetitions as you can do.

Watch your form. Keep your tailbone and the back of your head on the floor. You'll prevent your back from rounding, which would lessen the effect of the stretch.

SECTION 2: STANDING

HINGE

Works quadriceps, hip flexors

Kneel with your hands at your sides. Resist the urge to sit back and rest your weight on your heels. Your back should be straight and your knees bent at 90-degree angles. Keeping your head and back in line with your thighs, slowly lean back a few inches. Hold for 2 to 3 seconds, slowly return to the starting position, and repeat as many times as you can.

Watch your form. Don't bend at the waist or slouch forward doing so would steal effort from the fronts of your thighs.

STANDING HIP THRUST

Stretches hip flexors

Stand with your feet together, hands on your hips. Step forward with one foot so that your feet are a couple of feet apart. Keep your toes facing forward and your knees slightly bent. Gently push your pelvis forward until you feel a very mild stretch in your hips. Although this move seems subtle, don't overdo it: The hip flexors are attached inside the legs in such a way that it takes very little effort to stretch them. Hold the stretch for 5 seconds, then reverse leg positions and repeat.

Watch your form. Try to keep the same knee angle throughout the stretch.

SECTION 3: ON THE BOTTOM

LYING GLUTEAL BRIDGE

Works butt, hamstrings, abs, pelvic muscles

Lie on your back with your knees bent and your feet flat on the floor. Place your arms at your sides, palms facing down. Squeeze your glutes and slowly raise your butt off the floor until your body forms a straight line from your knees to your shoulders. Hold this position for 1 to 2 seconds, then slowly lower yourself back down and repeat the move as many times as you can.

Watch your form. Avoid looking at your waistline to check your posture. Keep your head flat on the floor and stare at the ceiling instead.

LYING CROSSOVER STRETCH

Stretches gluteal muscles

Lie on your back with your knees bent, feet flat on the floor. Slowly draw your right knee up to your chest. Grab the outside of the knee with your left hand and gently pull it toward left shoulder as far as is comfortable. Hold for 20 seconds, then lower the leg back to the starting position. Repeat the move, this time raising your left knee and pulling it toward your right shoulder.

Watch your form. Don't curl up as you bring your knee forward. Focus on keeping your head, shoulders, and back pressed flat against the floor.

KNEELING LEG CROSSOVER
Works gluteal muscles

SOCK SLIDE
Works shoulders, chest, triceps, lower back, abs

Get on all fours with your hands and knees shoulder-width apart and your head facing the floor. Straighten your right leg behind you, angling it to the right, with your toes touching the floor. This is the starting position. Now raise your right leg up and over your left leg, then lower it until your right foot touches the floor just outside your left foot. Reverse the motion to get back to the starting position and repeat as many times as you can. Switch positions to work your left leg.

Watch your form. Keep your spine straight throughout the move.

For this move, you need to be in socks on a slippery floor surface. Assume the pushup position, with your hands flat on the floor, shoulder-width apart, arms and legs straight, and feet together. Keeping your hands in place, slowly slide your body back until your nose is pointing down at the space between your hands. Next, slowly slide your body forward until your belly is almost over your hands. Continue moving backward and forward as many times as you can.

Watch your form. Keep your arms straight, abs in, and back flat.

Use Your Head

BY MIKE MEJIA, MS, CSCS

In this workout, you'll perform a power move first in each superset to prepare your nervous system to hoist heavier weights in the subsequent exercise. The result: greater strength gains. In each pair of moves, do six repetitions of each exercise without resting between exercises. Complete two rounds of every superset, resting for 2 minutes after each.

Superset 1

Plyometric pushup: Assume the standard pushup position. Quickly lower yourself to the floor, then push back up with enough force so your hands leave the floor. Land and immediately go into the next repetition.

Dumbbell bench press: Lie on a bench, holding a pair of heavy dumbbells with your arms extended over your chest and your palms facing your feet. Slowly lower the weights to the outside of your chest. Pause, then push them back up.

Superset 2

Explosive stepup: Stand with your right foot on a sturdy step or bench and your left foot flat on the floor. Keeping your torso upright, push hard off the bench to thrust yourself in the air. Cycle your legs so your left foot lands softly on the bench and your right foot lands on the floor.

Alternating dumbbell stepup: Holding dumbbells, stand with a bench in front of you. Step up with one foot, then back down. Repeat with the other leg. That's one repetition.

Superset 3

V-up: Lie on the floor with your legs straight and arms extended. Contract your abs to lift your torso and arms off the floor as you bring your legs toward you. Touch your toes with your hands at the top of the movement, then return to the starting position.

Weighted stability-ball situp: Lie back on a stability ball, holding a dumbbell with both hands against your chest. Curl up, stopping just short of upright. Slowly lower yourself to the starting position.

Training Tips

I'd like to start lifting, but my schedule only frees up after 9:00 p.m. Is it okay to work out this late at night?

If 9:00 p.m. is your only time, then it's the best time. You may feel slightly more energized for a couple of hours after you work out, but you also might get a deeper night's sleep than usual. If you're too alert, try to tweak your day so you can work out just before you need the most energy.

Should I wear a weight belt every time I lift heavy weights?

No. Olympic lifters and power lifters don't even wear weight belts— except when they near competition weights— because they need to develop core strength. So do you. First, aim to improve stability in your shoulders, torso, and hips in your workouts. As you gain strength, your core will become solid enough to handle heavier weights and more complex exercises without a weight belt.

I started lifting weights 4 months ago and gained 10 pounds in the first 3 months. Then, nothing. What happened?

Your body wised up and adapted to the punishment. To keep growing, start building muscle outside the gym—with nutrition and lifestyle choices. Bolster your workout with small meals or snacks before and after and continue to eat frequently throughout the day. In the weight room, for 3 weeks make your sets last longer than 40 seconds (to gain size), then keep them under 25 seconds for the next 3 weeks (to build strength). Continue to alternate between these approaches, and you'll soon break out of that holding pattern.

I work out in the morning. How long should I wait after eating to hit the gym? My stomach needs the blood to help with digestion, right?

The larger the meal (and the more fat or protein in it), the longer the wait. After a typical oatmeal-and-OJ breakfast, a 30- to 45-minute wait should suffice. You'll have to use trial and error to test your tolerance. But don't exercise on an empty stomach. Raising your blood sugar with a banana, a few bites of a sports bar, or a sports drink is much better than nothing.

Is there an exercise I can do to stop my slouching?

The best way to correct bad posture is to practice good posture. Consciously lift your chest when you walk and look straight ahead, not down. Also, strengthen your postural muscles, including your abs, your back, and the smaller muscles surrounding your hips, so they don't fatigue as the day wears on.

Begin by stretching your hamstrings and hip flexors. When these muscles are tight, they can cause strain on the lower back. Then try this move from Houston-based strength coach Carter Hays, CSCS. Do two or three sets of 12 repetitions.

Drop to your hands and knees, arms straight below your shoulders, knees under your hips. Stare between your hands. Lift your left arm and right leg until they're parallel to the floor. Hold for a count of four, lower them, and repeat with your opposite arm and leg. That's one repetition.

How can I build my chest quickly?

Use this tri set—three moves performed one after another without rest. It keeps consistent tension on your chest muscles to spur growth. Do 12 repetitions of each. Rest 90 seconds after the last move and repeat two or three times.

Swiss-ball alternating chest press: Lie faceup on a Swiss ball with your back against the ball and your feet flat on the floor. Hold a pair of dumbbells over your chest with straight arms. Lower the weight in your right hand to the side of your chest while keeping your left arm

straight. Pause, then press the weight back up and repeat with your left arm. That's one repetition.

Lunging cable chest fly: Stand between the stacks of a cable crossover station and grab a stirrup handle in each hand from the high pulleys. As you step forward with your left leg, pull the handles together so they meet in front of your chest. Pause when your right knee is about an inch off the floor and your left thigh is parallel to the floor. Return to the starting position and repeat with your right leg forward.

Decline Swiss-ball pushup: Assume the standard pushup position, but with your shins resting on a Swiss ball and your hands on the floor. Leading with your chest, lower your body until your arms form 90-degree angles. Then push back up to the starting position.

What's the difference between a pulled muscle and a torn one?

The difference is in severity. A "pulled" muscle is torn, but the tears are microscopic. With a "torn" muscle, you can actually see a deformity, and there may be swelling, bruising, and acute pain.

A pulled muscle can be painful when stressed and typically requires icing and rest for 1 to 3 weeks. One sign of a tear is a difficulty or inability to fully contract your muscle. Tears also require rest and ice but often surgery and rehab, too. When in doubt, call the doc.

MUSCLE
UP

Six hundred and fifty. That's the number of muscles in a man's body. Six hundred and fifty muscles to press, pull, lift, lower. Six hundred and fifty muscles to mow the lawn, swing a golf club, pick up a baby, caress a lady, and the millions of other things you do each and every day. Six hundred and fifty muscles to build to make you stronger, faster, harder, better.

Yet, while most men believe they know their way around a weight room, the truth is that one in three of us has dropped a weight on himself. Ouch. Many men aren't working out as efficiently—or effectively—as they could be. But the goal of 70 percent of guys who work out is to look more ripped. So we know your intentions are great.

In this section, we'll help you achieve that goal. First, we dispel the five biggest muscle myths. Then we clue you in on how to use combination lifts to build strength. Just in case your workout feels a bit stale, we'll pump it up with 10 super-charging tips.

And once you're armed with this information and put to the test, we're sure that all 650 of your muscles will be in their best shape ever.

BY MICHAEL MEJIA,
MS, CSCS

Update Your Workout

Is your workout past its
sell-by date? Here's how to
bring it into the 21st century

In a hospital, using outdated information is considered malpractice; in a gym, it's standard operating procedure. Don't believe it? Take a look at today's most sacred lifting guidelines, and you'll find that some originated in the '40s and '50s, a time when castration was a cutting-edge treatment for prostate cancer and endurance exercise was believed harmful to women. What's worse, other, more recent recommendations regarding exercise form have been negated by new research yet are still commonly prescribed by fitness professionals.

Chances are, these are the same rules you lift by right now. That means your workout is long past due for a 21st-century overhaul. This isn't to say that your current plan doesn't work. After all, at its most basic level, building muscle is simple: Pick up a heavy weight, put it down, repeat. But improve the details and avoid mistakes, and you'll build more muscle in less time with less risk of injury. Put a check next to today's date; it marks the official expiration of your old workout.

Age-Old Advice: "Do 8 to 12 Reps"

The claim: It's the optimal repetition range for building muscle.

The origin: In 1954, Ian MacQueen, MD, an English surgeon and competitive bodybuilder, published a scientific paper in which he recommended a moderately high number of repetitions for muscle growth.

The truth: This approach places muscles under a medium amount of tension for a medium amount of time, making it both effective for and detrimental to maximum gains.

A quick science lesson: Higher tension—aka heavier weights—induces the type of growth in which the muscle fibers grow larger, leading to the best gains in strength; longer tension time, on the other hand, boosts size by increasing the energy-producing structures around the fibers, improving muscular endurance.

The classic prescription of 8 to 12 repetitions strikes a balance between the two. But by using that scheme all the time, you miss out on the greater tension levels that come with heavier weights and fewer repetitions, as well as the longer tension time achieved with lighter weights and higher repetitions.

The new standard: Vary your repetition range—adjusting weights accordingly—so that you stimulate every type of muscle growth. Try this method for a month, performing three full-body sessions a week: Do five repetitions per set in your first workout, 10 reps per set in your second workout, and 15 per set in your third.

Age-Old Advice: "Do Three Sets of Each Exercise"

The claim: This provides the ideal workload for achieving the fastest muscle gains.

The origin: In 1948, a physician named Thomas Delorme reported in the *Archives of Physical Medicine* that performing three sets of 10 repetitions was as effective at improving leg strength as 10 sets of 10 repetitions.

The truth: There's nothing wrong with—or magical about—doing three sets. But the number of sets you perform shouldn't be determined by a 50-year-old default recommendation. Here's a rule of thumb: The more repetitions of an exercise you do, the fewer sets you should perform, and vice versa. This keeps the total number of reps nearly equal, no matter how many repetitions make up each set.

The new standard: Use this chart to determine the number of sets you should do.

Reps	13–20	8–12	4–7	1–3
Sets	1–2	2–3	4–5	6–10

Age-Old Advice: "Do Three or Four Exercises per Muscle Group"

The claim: This ensures that you work all the fibers of the target muscle.

The origin: Arnold, circa 1966.

The truth: You'll waste a lot of time. Here's why: Schwarzenegger's 4-decade-old recommendation is almost always combined with, "Do three sets of 8 to 12 repetitions." That means you'll complete up to 144 repetitions for each muscle group. Trouble is, if you can perform even close to 100 repetitions for any muscle group, you're not working hard enough. Think of it this way: The harder you train, the less time you'll be able to sustain that level of effort. For example, many men can run for an hour if they jog slowly, but you'd be hard-pressed to find anyone who could do high-intensity sprints—without a major decrease in performance—for that period of time. And once performance starts to decline, you've achieved all the muscle-building benefits you can for that muscle group.

The new standard: Instead of focusing on the number of different exercises you do, shoot for a total number of repetitions between 25 and 50. That could mean five sets of five repetitions of one exercise (25 repetitions) or one set of 15 repetitions of two or three exercises (30 to 45 repetitions).

Age-Old Advice: "Never Let Your Knees Go Past Your Toes"

The claim: Allowing your knees to move too far forward during exercises such as the squat and lunge places dangerous shearing forces on your knee ligaments.

The origin: A 1978 study at Duke University found that keeping the lower leg as vertical as possible during the squat reduced shearing forces on the knee.

The truth: Leaning forward too much is more likely to cause injury. In 2003, University of Memphis researchers confirmed that knee stress was 28 percent higher when the knees were allowed to move past the toes during the squat. But the researchers also found a countereffect: Hip stress increased nearly 1,000 percent when forward movement of the knee was restricted. The reason: The squatters had to lean their torsos farther forward. And that's a problem, because forces that act on the hip are transferred to

Perfect Form

Iron out lifting flaws to get the most from these major muscle-makers.

Barbell squat:

Don't lean forward and bend down a few inches. This puts excessive pressure on your lower back while increasing the stress on your knees.

Do sit back (keeping your torso as upright as possible) as you lower your body until your thighs are at least parallel to the floor.

Barbell bench press:

Don't overarch your back or lift your heels off the floor.

Do keep your back naturally arched (the way it is when you first lie down on the bench) and your feet flat on the floor at all times.

Chinup:

Don't stop part way down or use momentum to pull yourself back up.

Do lower your body until your arms are straight, pause, and then pull yourself back up.

Dumbbell shoulder press:

Don't clank the weights together at the top of the movement; it increases risk of a shoulder-impingement injury without benefiting your muscles.

Do push the weights straight above your shoulders.

the lower back, a more frequent site of injury than the knees.

The new standard: Focus more on your upper body and less on knee position. By trying to keep your torso as upright as possible as you perform squats (and lunges), you'll reduce the stress on your hips and back. Two tips for staying upright: Before squatting, squeeze your shoulder blades together and hold them that way; and as you squat, try to keep your forearms perpendicular to the floor.

Age-Old Advice: "When You Lift Weights, Draw in Your Abs"

The claim: You'll increase the support to your spine, reducing the risk of back injuries.

The origin: In 1999, researchers in Australia found that some men with back pain had a slight delay in activating their transverse abdominis, a deep abdominal muscle that's part of the musculature that maintains spine stability. As a result, many fitness professionals began instructing their clients to try to pull their belly buttons to their spines—which engages the transverse abdominis—as they performed exercises.

The truth: "The research was accurate, but the interpretation by many researchers and therapists wasn't," says Stuart McGill, PhD, author of *Ultimate Back Fitness and Performance* and widely recognized as the world's top researcher on the spine. That's because muscles work in teams to stabilize your spine, and the most valuable players change depending on the exercise, says Dr. McGill. Read: The transverse abdominis isn't always the quarterback. In fact, for any given exercise, your body automatically activates the muscles that are most needed for spine support. So focusing only on your transverse abdominis can overrecruit the wrong muscles and underrecruit the right ones. This not only increases injury risk but reduces the amount of weight you can lift.

The new standard: If you want to give your back a supporting hand, simply "brace" your abs as if you were about to be punched in the gut, but don't draw them in. "This activates all three layers of the abdominal wall, improving both stability and performance," says Dr. McGill.

PEAK
performance

A 5-Day, Full-Body Workout

This 4-day split routine will divide up your lifting days without leading to overtraining.

Monday: Upper-body pushing exercises (bench presses, military presses) and lower-body pulling movements (deadlifts, leg curls)

Tuesday: Lower-body pushing moves (squats, lunges) and upper-body pulling exercises (pullups, rows)

Wednesday: Regeneration day—some cardio, foam-roll massage, and active flexibility exercises

Thursday: Upper-body pushing exercises (bench presses, military presses) and lower-body pulling movements (deadlifts, leg curls)

Friday: Lower-body pushing moves (squats, lunges) and upper-body pulling exercises (pullups, rows)

Another option: Do total-body weight training on Monday, Wednesday, and Friday, and focus on cardio regeneration, stability, and flexibility work on Tuesday and Saturday.

Go for the Combo

Use these combination lifts to build strength, shed fat, and look your best

BY ROBERT DOS REMEDIOS, CSCS

Before yet another ugly fitness trend takes hold, I hereby command all men who are performing sumo squats while curling 10-pound dumbbells to stop—and listen up. I don't blame you. Maybe you've heard trainers say that adding an arm curl to a squat "gives you more bang for your buck!" These men are butchers. Combination exercises—two or more moves blended together—are intended to work a ton of muscle mass and save time. I use them with every athlete I train, because they build muscle, burn fat, and shake up stale routines. But the key is choosing exercises that don't limit the amount of weight you can use or disturb a movement's flow. Here are three of my favorite combination routines. You can use any of them as your total-body workout three times a week. And feel free to mix it up. Just don't let me catch you with a pair of 12s, doing a deadlift with a triceps kickback . . .

There are three types of combination exercises: pure, hybrid, and complex. Here's a workout for each.

Pure Combination: Get Stronger

A pure combination is two or more exercises done back-to-back, with a distinct pause between movements. The brief pause allows you to reset your feet, take a breath, and ultimately handle a greater load to build strength and power.

The workout: Do five repetitions of each pure combination below. Complete three sets, resting 2 minutes between sets.

CLEAN PULL + POWER SHRUG

Grab a bar with an overhand grip (palms facing thighs) and place your feet shoulder-width apart. Keeping your back flat and arms straight, squeeze your glutes and push your feet against the floor as you straighten your legs, rise onto your toes, and shrug your shoulders.

Pause, then push your hips back and lower the bar to your knees.

Next, forcefully push your hips forward and shrug your shoulders toward your ears.

Lower the bar to the floor. That's one repetition.

DUMBBELL ROMANIAN DEADLIFT + HANG CLEAN + PUSH PRESS

Stand holding dumbbells in front of your thighs, knees slightly bent.

Push your hips back to lower the weights to your shins.

Return to the starting position. Pause, then forcefully pull the weights upward as you dip under and "catch" them in front of your

shoulders. The weights should roll to your fingers, and your elbows should point forward.

Stand, then pause. Bend your knees slightly, then straighten your legs and press the dumbbells overhead. Lower the weights to the starting position.

BACK SQUAT + GOOD MORNING + PUSH PRESS

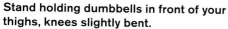

Hold a bar across the back of your shoulders with an overhand grip, feet shoulder-width apart.

Keeping your back straight, lower your body as if sitting, until your thighs are parallel to the floor.

Press up, then pause. Next, bend at the hips as far as you can without losing the natural curve in your spine.

Contract your glutes and push your hips forward to stand. Pause, bend slightly at the knees, and drive up with your legs, thrusting the weight overhead. Return to the starting position.

Hybrid Combination: Perform Better

A hybrid exercise is a blend of two or more movements that merge. By flowing from one plane of movement to another—up and down, side to side, and twisting across your body—these sequences mimic the unpredictability of sports, so they help you move with more quickness and agility on the court or field.

The workout: Do three sets of 8 to 10 repetitions of each hybrid exercise below, resting 1 to 2 minutes between sets.

FRONT SQUAT TO PUSH PRESS

Stand holding a bar on the front of your shoulders, with your elbows pointing straight ahead.

Lower your body until your thighs are parallel to the floor.

As you push back up to the starting position, press the bar overhead. Lower the bar to your shoulders and immediately sink into your next squat.

ROTATIONAL REACH-AND-TOUCH LUNGE TO CURL AND PRESS

Stand holding dumbbells at your sides.

With your left leg, lunge forward and to the left at a 45-degree angle. As you bend your knee to lower your body, reach with both arms and touch the weights to the floor, one on each side of your left foot.

As you push yourself up, curl the weights to your shoulders.

Then press them overhead. Return to the starting position. That's one repetition. Repeat for a total of eight to 10, alternating legs as you go.

Complex Combination: Look Leaner

The next combination is called a complex, but it's actually quite simple. You'll complete a set (10 reps) of one exercise, then move to the next exercise in the complex. Since each exercise begins in a similar position—standing with dumbbells, for instance—you don't waste time setting up between exercises. The result: You accomplish more work in a shorter time, so your heart rate stays elevated, and you burn a lot of calories.

DUMBBELL SQUAT + PUSH PRESS + ROW

Stand holding dumbbells at your sides.

Lower your body until your thighs are parallel to the floor.

Then push back up and repeat 10 times. Without pausing, bring the dumbbells to your shoulders and hold them with your palms forward. Dip down at the knees.

Then straighten your legs and thrust the weights overhead. Do 10 repetitions.

Next, bend forward at the waist until your back is almost parallel to the floor. Pull the weights up to your rib cage, lower them, and repeat for 10 repetitions.

PEAK performance

Big Muscles on Any Budget

Impressive muscles don't have to cost an arm and a leg. Here's how to bulk up, no matter what your bankroll.

If you have $100, buy: A Stability Ball Plus ($23; www.performbetter.com). Made of burst-resistant vinyl, it comes in four sizes and can hold up to 600 pounds. Also pick up a pair of Pro-Style dumbbells ($70; www.performbetter.com).

If you have another $160, add: The HF-4163 flat bench from Hoist Fitness, which adjusts for flat, incline, and decline exercises—and collapses to fit under a bed ($160; www.hoistfitness.com).

If you have another $400, buy: A pair of Nautilus SelecTech Dumbbells. Twist the end caps to transform each dumbbell from 5 to 52.5 pounds and weights in between ($400; www.nautilus.com).

If you have another $1,210, add: A power rack/cage from Tuff Stuff ($550; www.tuffstuff.net) and a 300-pound weight set with bar from Ivanko weights ($660; www.ivanko.com).

BARBELL HIGH PULL + FRONT SQUAT + ROMANIAN DEADLIFT

Hold a bar with a shoulder-width grip in front of your knees. Your knees should be bent, hips back, and back flat.

Straighten your hips and legs and rise onto your toes as you pull the bar up to just below your chin. Do 10 reps.

Then place the bar on the front of your shoulders, with your elbows pointing straight ahead.

Lower your body until your thighs are parallel to the floor, then press up.

After 10 reps, stand with your knees slightly bent, your arms straight, and the bar in front of your thighs.

Push your hips back until the bar reaches shin level, then push back up and repeat for 10 reps.

DUMBBELL LUNGE + PUSHUP + CORE ROW

Stand holding dumbbells at your sides.

Stride forward with your left leg until your left thigh is parallel to the floor, then press up. Alternate legs and perform 10 lunges with each leg.

Next, get into pushup position with your hands resting on the dumbbells and placed beneath your shoulders, your palms facing each other.

Do 10 pushups.

From the pushup position (arms straight), pull one dumbbell off the floor and toward your body with your right arm until your elbow is higher than your back. Return the weight to the floor and repeat with your left arm. Do 10 with each arm.

BY MYATT MURPHY

Pump Up Your Workout

10 ways to supercharge
a boring gym session

We should have a "refresh" button for everything: a bitter coworker, a lame bar scene, the National Hockey League. Just a click or two could give us instant improvement.

Same with tired workouts. Maybe yours has frozen up like a gym version of Windows 95. You may think you have to reboot. Instead, all you need are a few tweaks for a faster, more enjoyable, more effective workout.

Take a typical guy's stale routine: treadmill for 5 minutes, then bench presses until someone asks if he's almost done—in which case he's suddenly on his last set. Next, a few rows, curls, and crunches, then a quick toe touch, and he's out.

You can do better, beginning with your warmup. "Most men warm up with a few minutes of light cycling or jogging," says Brad Jordan, NSCA-CPT, a personal trainer in Dayton, Ohio. That's fine if all you plan to do in your workout is lower-body exercise. But an upper-body workout demands something that's more in sync with your plans. "Switch your warmup to jumping rope, rowing lightly, or using any cardio machine, like an elliptical trainer, that makes you pump your arms," Jordan says.

As for the rest of your routine . . . stop calling it routine. Refresh it—and yourself—with these moves.

Start with Your Hamstrings

"Most men do the exercises they like first and save the ones they know they hate for last," says Steve Lischin, NASM-CPT. "Toward the end of a workout, they either put little effort into these exercises or just skip them entirely." Performing your workout in the opposite order can give muscles you tend to overlook (such as your hamstrings) the attention they deserve. And saving your favorites for last can help you recharge when your energy level is in decline.

Stretch Between Sets

"Don't stretch only when your muscles feel tight," says Jordan. Stretching the muscles you're working not only helps them stay loose but can also increase your range of motion, allowing you to work more muscle fibers with each additional set.

Take a Coffee Break

Anytime you draw your legs toward your midsection—reverse crunches, V-ups—you emphasize the lower portion of your abs. These moves also stress your hip flexors, the muscles at the front of your thighs. When these muscles are involved, your abs exert less than full effort, and you end up with tight hip flexors.

Overcome this tendency by pretending there's a cup of coffee resting just below your belly button. Before bringing your legs up each time, imagine tilting that cup toward your legs first. "This redirects your body positioning, so the effort stays concentrated on the lower abs," says Len Kravitz,

PhD, coordinator of exercise science at the University of New Mexico.

Close Your Eyes While Exercising

This helps you visualize the muscles you're working, which is especially helpful for posterior muscle groups like your back, hamstrings, and butt. (Exceptions are allowed when that brunette happens to walk by.) Also try closing your eyes during any exercise that involves balance, such as a one-legged squat. "It challenges the neuromuscular system and helps you establish better balance," says Carter Hays, CSCS, a Houston-based personal trainer. "It's actually harder closing just one eye than both eyes; it's weird."

Change Your Inclination

Rather than do three sets of dumbbell presses followed by three sets of incline presses, combine the two exercises. Start with one set of chest presses on a flat bench. Then raise the bench one notch from the flat position—to about 15 to 20 degrees—for your second set. Continue raising the angle one notch per set, stopping at the notch before vertical. "This lets you exhaust more muscle fibers by working your chest through five or six different angles instead of just the basic two," says Wayne Westcott, PhD, a Massachusetts-based exercise researcher. You'll actually end up doing fewer sets, so you'll save time, too.

Get Twisted

During the standard single-arm dumbbell row, your palm faces in as you raise and

PAINkiller

I have a nagging hip problem. A coworker recommended a therapist who practices "ART." What is this, and is it effective?

ART, or active release techniques, treats muscle, tendon, ligament, and nerve problems by combining deep-muscle massage with specific movements that the patient makes. In the case of a biceps injury, for example, the ART therapist will have you flex your biceps while she presses on a spot on the muscle; then she'll direct you to extend the elbow. And yes, it can hurt. The manual pressure helps break up microtraumas and scar tissue, which accelerates the recovery process. ART can be a very effective soft-tissue therapy for hip injuries, as long as you have a skilled practitioner doing the treatment. To find a therapist, seek out recommendations from the staff at local gyms and sports-training facilities. For more information about ART, go to www.activerelease.com.

lower the weight along the side of your chest. To get more out of the move, rotate your wrist inward 180 degrees as you lower the dumbbell so that your thumb points behind you when your arm is completely straight. This rotation helps adduct the scapula, working the back through a fuller range of motion for added strength and size.

Stop and Go

Instead of raising and lowering the weight in one continuous motion, pause for a second about halfway up, continue the movement, and then pause again about halfway down. "In a set of eight to 12 repetitions, you'll add only 16 to 24 seconds to each set, but you'll be able to exhaust your muscles faster using less weight," says Lischin. This tactic works great with shoulder presses, lateral raises, and bent-over lateral raises.

Lower the Weight with One Leg

Your muscles are much stronger during the eccentric phase of an exercise—when the weight is being lowered. With leg presses, leg curls, and leg extensions, consider the "two up, one down" option. Press or curl the weight up with both legs, then slowly lower it using only one leg. This lets you work your muscles even harder in the same amount of time without constantly needing to change the weight, says Dr. Westcott.

Spread 'Em

Change your hand spacing with each set of barbell curls, instead of keeping them placed at shoulder width for all your repetitions. "Spreading your hands a few inches farther out stresses more of the inner portion of your biceps, while bringing your hands in a few inches builds more of the outer part," says Lischin. Or, try switching from the standard shoulder-width grip on a barbell to an angled position with an EZ-curl bar.

Run the Rack

Save time on the last dumbbell exercise in your workout. Instead of doing three sets of shoulder presses, biceps curls, or any dumbbell move, start with a weight that's about 50 percent of what you usually use to do 10 to 12 repetitions. Perform the exercise six times, then quickly grab the weight that's one increment heavier. Continue working your way up in weight until you finally find one that you can't lift six times using proper technique. Then reverse this process by grabbing a slightly lighter weight and completing as many repetitions as possible, even if you can manage only a few. Keep moving down the rack until you're left using the lightest set of dumbbells possible.

BY MYATT MURPHY

Build a Fat-Burning Body

Lose flab and reveal muscle with this compound-exercise workout

To burn fat, take a two-part approach. First, work as many muscle groups as possible. Compound exercises that work multiple muscles across multiple joints are "more effective than isolation exercises at burning fat," says Len Kravitz, PhD, coordinator of exercise science at the University of New Mexico. The more muscle fibers you utilize, the more lean muscle tissue you'll develop, which will really boost your metabolism. Second, you need to mix cardiovascular exercise with your weight training. Follow this plan and you'll build a body that has no choice but to melt fat all day, every day, for a leaner, stronger physique.

The Payoff

Great definition! Going for a leaner look may seem as if you're sacrificing size, but losing body fat can make your body look bigger. Strip away excess fat and uncover your muscles for a more defined look—making your muscles appear much larger.

Instant energy! Training aerobically causes your body to produce more adenosine tri-phosphate (ATP), a molecule that carries energy to your body's cells. Having more ATP boosts your stamina on the playing field, between the sheets, and throughout the day.

More time! A workout composed of super-sets and trisets—exercises performed back-to-back without rest—is a faster-paced routine than traditional straight sets with rest after each move. This means you'll shave minutes off your workout while your muscles receive the same level of stress.

The Workout

This array of classic compound exercises performed in superset fashion adds up to a full-body plan with a few twists—literally. Many of the moves require you to turn the weights as you lift. These slight variations can help bring even more muscle fibers into play.

To maximize the fat-burning effect, you have to minimize the time you spend rest-ing. For each superset or triset, do 10 to 15 repetitions of the first exercise, then imme-diately proceed to the next move in the pair or trio. So perform the squat immediately after the lunge; do the bench press, row, and Arnold press one after another; do the dip immediately after the curl; and perform the double crunch as its own set. Rest only as long as assigned between sets.

Maintaining this fast pace allows you to do more work in a shorter period of time. That way, you'll always have enough time after your weight routine for the cardio work required to burn more calories and shed extra fat.

Your body can become a fat-burning machine if you build large muscle groups like your back, chest, quadriceps, ham-strings, and gluteal muscles. Focus on these and you'll work more muscle fibers than if you targeted smaller ones, and you'll add lean muscle to your frame. More lean mus-cle means a more effective resting metabolic rate. That's why every muscle plays a part in building a body that burns fat.

The 4-Week Program

TIME PERIOD	WEEK 1	WEEK 2	WEEK 3	WEEK 4
Create your routine by . . .	Doing the exercises in the order shown	Doing the exercises in the order shown	Doing the exercises in the order shown	Doing both moves from all 4 sections
Sets of each exercise or stretch	2	2	2	2
Your total workout should be . . .	16 sets	16 sets	24 sets	24 sets
Rest between supersets:	15–30 seconds	15 seconds	15–30 seconds	30 seconds
Do this workout	Twice a week	Three times a week	Twice a week	Three times a week
Do cardio training immediately afterward for at least	15–20 minutes	20–25 minutes	25–30 minutes	25–30 minutes
Do cardio training between workouts at least	1 day	1 day	2 days	2 days

LOWER-BODY SUPERSET

STEP LUNGE
Legs

Holding dumbbells at your sides, stand about 3 feet from a step with your feet hip-width apart.

Stride forward onto the step with your left foot so that your left thigh ends up parallel to the floor. Push yourself back to the starting position and repeat the exercise, this time stepping forward with your right leg.

Watch your form. Stepping onto just your toes or the ball of your foot requires more effort from your calves, so they'll tire faster than your other leg muscles.

ARNOLD PRESS

Front deltoids, middle deltoids, triceps, upper trapezius

Stand holding a pair of dumbbells in front of you at chest height with an underhand grip (palms facing you).

As you push the weights overhead, rotate your arms so that your palms face forward at the top of the movement. Pause at the top, then slowly lower the weights back down, rotating your wrists as you go, so that your palms face you again.

Watch your form: Slowly twist your wrists throughout the move. The top and bottom of the exercise are the only points at which the weights should not turn.

SINGLE SET

FIGURE-FOUR DOUBLE CRUNCH

Upper and lower abs

Lie flat on your back with your knees bent, feet flat on the floor. Place your hands on your head behind your ears. Rest your right ankle on your left knee and raise your left foot a couple of inches. This is the starting position.

Slowly curl yourself forward as you bring your left knee toward you. Pause, lower yourself (keeping your left foot off the floor), and repeat for a set. Switch positions so that your left ankle lies across your right knee and repeat the move for another set.

Watch your form: Bring your knee only slightly toward you.

Watch your form: Spend at least 2 to 3 seconds going up and the same going down. Rushing can disrupt your balance and force you to stop.

Gain Practical Strength

BY MIKE MEJIA, MS, CSCS

Most "Get huge!" training plans develop big guns that fire blanks. You need useful muscle. This plan yields bulk and core strength. You'll build an injury-resistant platform and hoist heavier weights than usual, leading to big gains in size. Perform these exercises back-to-back in three circuits, resting for 2 minutes after each cycle.

Dumbbell deadlift: Stand with a heavy dumbbell on the floor beside each foot. Bend your knees and grab the weights with your palms facing in.

Keeping your head and chest up, your back arched naturally, and your torso leaning forward no more than 45 degrees, push your feet against the floor and stand up. Then lower yourself, maintaining the arch in your back.

Floor press: Grab a pair of heavy dumbbells and sit on the floor with your knees bent, feet on the floor. Lie down with your upper arms in contact with the floor and hold the dumbbells next to your shoulders, as if you were about to perform a bench press.

Press the weights up over your chest, then lower them.

Negative situp: Sit on the floor with your knees bent 90 degrees and hold a dumbbell with both hands close to your chest.

Take 5 or 6 seconds to lower your back toward the floor, one vertebra at a time. (Try not to increase speed as you get closer to the floor.) Sit back up using as little momentum as possible.

Training Tips

How much supplemental protein does a typical weight-lifting man really need to gain muscle?

No more than 30 grams per day, says Dave Grotto, RD, a *Men's Health* nutrition advisor. "Protein provides 4 calories per gram," he says. "So whatever our bodies aren't using will become extra baggage."

I know you're not supposed to eat before going to bed, but I have to work out at 11:00 p.m. What can I eat after my workout?

Just make sure you eat your last complete meal of the day an hour or two before your workout. A small postworkout, presnooze snack is fine. Try a cup of low-fat yogurt and a banana, or some cereal and an orange, or a protein shake. Then shower up and hit the sheets.

I'm a pretty laid-back guy, but when I'm lifting regularly, I get fired up and flip out a lot. I'm not juicing. Is there some way I can prevent this reaction?

It's adrenaline that's revving your motor. Cap your workout with a brief meditation. Forget the yoga mat and Half Lord of the Fishes pose—just take 20 slow, deep breaths, repeating a mantra (one word, like *calm, chill,* or *cheeseburger*—whatever helps you relax) each time you exhale. Do it sitting on a bench, on the floor, or just standing up.

Meditation spurs the brain's prefrontal cortex (the CEO up top), helping you rein in impulsive thoughts.

Even though I lift the same amount of weight on both sides, one arm is bigger than the other. What gives?

No need to join the circus; mismatched arms are not uncommon. "It largely has to do with whether you're right- or left-handed," says Steven Devor, PhD, a professor of exercise physiology at Ohio State University and a *Men's Health* advisor. For example, you'll use your nondominant arm to hold groceries while your more coordinated hand unlocks the door. After you favor one arm all day, every day—in addition to any weight training—the nondominant arm can outgrow the dominant one. At the gym, ditch the barbell and pick up dumbbells to avoid favoring one arm, especially when struggling to pull through those last few reps. "If you have a 30-pound dumbbell in each hand, each arm is lifting 30 pounds," says Dr. Devor. "You

can't get around that." Outside the gym, become a conscious carrier. "Think, *Okay, I'm going to carry my groceries with my smaller arm,*" says Dr. Devor. *"I'm going to provide more load on that arm than I normally do."*

My schedule allows me to lift in the morning, at lunch, or after work. When should I work out?

Your body functions best on a consistent schedule, so the most important thing is to choose a time and stick to it. If you're a morning person, an early workout might be best—before the demands of your day get in the way. You'll also be boosting your metabolism for a daylong surge in calorie burn. On the other hand, the lunch window helps break up the day and recharge your body and mind. Regardless of what time you work out, have a whey-isolate shooter beforehand and follow up with a postworkout recovery shake. You'll ensure that you're getting the most out of your workout.

What are a man's most neglected muscles?

The scapular retractors, a small set responsible for pulling your shoulder blades toward your

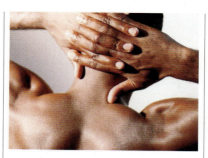

spine. Since most men focus on shoulder presses and lateral raises to build their shoulders and pullups and lat pulldowns for their backs, they rarely train their scapular retractors effectively. The result is poor shoulder stability. This, in turn, will make you weaker at every upper-body lift.

To remedy weak retractors, lie under a secure bar that's about 3 feet off the floor, grab it with a shoulder-width overhand grip, and hang at arm's length. Without bending your elbows, raise your body by squeezing your shoulder blades together. Pause for 2 to 3 seconds, relax, and repeat. Do two sets of eight to 10 repetitions, resting a minute between sets.

It seems like every time I start to make gains in my workouts, I end up getting hurt. Am I just injury-prone?

No, you're following a bad plan. First, make sure you're choosing

exercises and weights that allow you to maintain perfect technique. Second, try using dumbbells or cables, because they help correct any imbalances you've developed over time. Finally, include a supplemental routine that strengthens commonly weak areas like the glutes and scapular muscles.

I feel as if I'm wasting time in the gym during the summer. Would it kill me to knock off lifting for all of July and August?

Go for it. Being active outside can keep you in excellent health. Try mountain biking, hiking, basketball, waterskiing, and swimming. To stay in really great shape, find a balance by hitting the gym twice a week for 45 minutes to get in your big lifts (squats, bench presses) and by incorporating pushups, pullups, lunges, and plyometrics into your outdoor workouts.

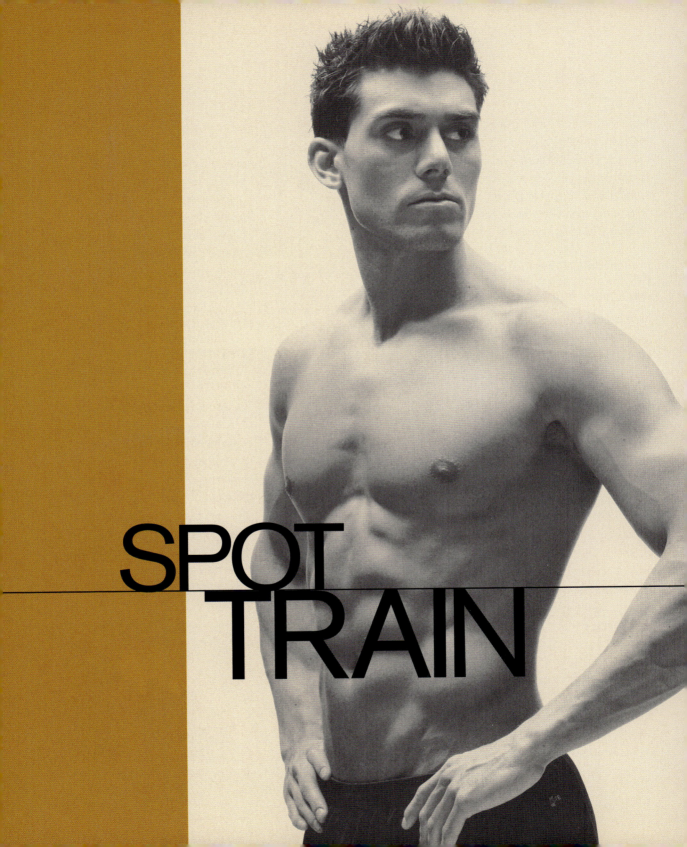

SPOT
TRAIN

In this section, let's pick apart your parts. Perhaps you have great broad shoulders, but your arms are lacking. Or you might have bulging biceps but an equally bulging belly. Maybe your belly is firm but your shoulders are sloping. We'd like to help you balance everything out.

First, we'll show you how to build bolder shoulders. Next, you'll arm yourself with stronger arms. Then our program will help you sculpt a strong, broad chest. Finally, use our plan to get the ultimate eight-pack—even better than a six-pack.

The payoff? Put it all together for increased strength, improved physique, extra power, more speed, a stronger grip, less pain, a trimmer waistline, better stamina, more balance, and even an edge in sports.

Read on to build your best body, one part at a time.

BY MYATT MURPHY

Here's how to strengthen
your core muscles for
the best body ever

Chisel a
Rock-Solid Core

Most men never bother to develop core strength. "Men tend to focus more on the muscles they can see, so they work on their six-packs, but the obliques, lower back, and hips are all part of the core," says Mike Huff, CSCS, coordinator of sports performance at the Michael W. Krzyzewski Human Performance Lab at Duke Medical Center. Focus on core muscles first, to gain the strength and stability to help you perform the real muscle-building moves. Proper training enables all the core muscles to work in sync, says Huff. "The only way to achieve that kind of synergy is through functional exercises that require those muscles to work together."

Don't confuse an ab routine with a core workout. A true core program develops dozens of muscles attached to the hips, pelvis, lower back, and abdominals. We'll focus on four muscle groups: the erector spinae, along the spinal column; the rectus abdominis, from the middle of your rib cage to your pubic bone; the obliques, alongside your waist; and the transverse abdominis, under your obliques.

The Payoff

Ultimate agility! Developed core muscles help you react faster and stronger and let your body distribute stress evenly and absorb shock effectively. Athletes who give these muscles proper attention will reap enhanced balance, body awareness, coordination, and flexibility.

Dominant power! The most effective exercises for developing power, such as deadlifts and squats, require a strong core to stabilize and protect the lower back. Conditioning the deep core muscles gives you the foundation needed to lift more weight with less risk of injury.

Perfect posture! The more centered your spine is in relation to the rest of your body, the more erect you'll sit and stand. Strong lower-back and abdominal muscles help you run with proper technique, sustain a long commute, even sit at a desk all day. Clothes fit better, and you appear taller, slimmer, and more confident.

Long-term weight loss! Developing your core helps you perform daily tasks with less effort and fatigue. This means you'll have more energy to burn in the gym or on the field, and less time on the sidelines from early exhaustion or injury.

The Workout

This program strengthens major and minor muscles at the same time. Many of the exercises involve rotation of the spine, which engages more of the erector spinae and the internal and external obliques. Your core muscles work all day long, so they're resistant to fatigue. That means you won't need many rest days on this program.

The plan can be a separate workout three or four times a week. But if you weight-train regularly, put it at the end of your routine twice a week—preferably on the day you perform squats or deadlifts. This will make it easier to exhaust your core muscles. Don't worry about the number of reps; concentrate on form and on going slowly.

The 4-Week Program

TIME PERIOD	WEEK 1	WEEK 2	WEEK 3	WEEK 4
Create your routine by:	Picking 1 move from section A, 1 from B, and 2 from C	Combining the 4 moves you didn't use during week 1	Doing all 8 moves in the order shown	Doing all 8 moves in the order shown
Sets of each exercise:	2	2	1–2	1–2
Your total workout should be:	8 sets	8 sets	8–16 sets	8–16 sets
Repetitions per set:	As many as you can do with perfect form	As many as you can do with perfect form	As many as you can do with perfect form	As many as you can do with perfect form
Speed of each repetition:	At least 2 seconds up and 2 seconds down	At least 2 seconds up and 2 seconds down	At least 2 seconds up and 2 seconds down	At least 2 seconds up and 2 seconds down
Rest between sets:	30 seconds	30 seconds	15–30 seconds	15–30 seconds
Do this workout:	Once or twice a week	2 or 3 times a week	2 or 3 times a week	3 or 4 times a week

SECTION A

SIDE BRIDGE

Obliques, shoulders

Lie on your left side with your legs and feet together, your right hand on your right hip, and your left forearm on the floor so your elbow is beneath your shoulder.

Raise your hips until your body forms a straight line from shoulder to ankle. Pause, slowly lower your body, and repeat, then switch to your right side.

Watch your form: Keep your neck in line with your torso as much as possible to avoid straining your trapezius and neck muscles.

SWISS-BALL TWIST

Obliques, shoulders to waist

Lie on a Swiss ball so your head, shoulders, and upper back touch its surface. Your knees should be bent, your feet flat on the floor. Cross your arms over your chest.

Slowly twist your upper body to the left until you're lying on your left shoulder. Slowly rotate back to the starting position. Repeat the move, this time rolling to the right.

Watch your form: Resist the urge to tilt your head excessively up to the side or down to look at the ball or the floor. Your head, neck, and spine should form a straight line and remain that way.

SECTION B

REACH-AND-TWIST HYPEREXTENSION

Lower back, erector spinae, obliques

Lie on a hyperextension bench with your ankles under the ankle pads. Hold a light medicine ball to your chest and lean forward until your upper body is almost perpendicular to the floor.

Slowly raise your torso, twisting your upper body to the right and extending the ball away from you until your arms are straight. Rise until your body is just past parallel to the floor. Reverse the motion, then repeat, twisting and reaching to the left.

Watch your form: Go slowly: 3 seconds up and 3 down. Rushing uses momentum and increases risk of injury.

SWISS-BALL TWISTING HYPEREXTENSION

Lower back, erector spinae, obliques

Lie facedown on a Swiss ball with your waist on top of it. Place your feet against a wall or under something sturdy. Cross your arms and bend forward until your upper body covers the ball.

Slowly raise your torso off the ball, gently twisting to the right, until your torso is slightly past parallel to the floor. Lower yourself and repeat, this time twisting to the left.

Watch your form: At the top of the move, the top of your pelvis should rest on the Swiss ball. If you can feel the ball against your lower abs, you're not forward enough on it.

SECTION C

SWISS-BALL KNEE TUCK

Transverse abdominis, obliques, rectus abdominis

Assume the pushup position with your shins on a Swiss ball and your hands on the floor, shoulder-width apart and beneath your shoulders.

Keeping your head down and your abs drawn in, slowly pull your knees toward your chest. (The ball will roll slightly forward.) Try to keep your hips down to maintain the stress on your abdominals. Pause, then straighten your legs to roll the ball back out behind you.

Watch your form: Keep your belly button pulled in toward your spine. This engages your transverse abdominis, which helps protect your back.

CABLE CHOP

Obliques, transverse abdominis

Use a weight that allows you to do no more than 12 to 15 repetitions. Stand with your right shoulder toward a high-pulley cable station and grab the rope or handle with both hands.

Keeping your toes forward and knees bent, slowly rotate to your left as you draw your arms across and down. Pause when your hands are above your left thigh, then slowly reverse the motion. After a set, repeat the move with your left shoulder facing the stack.

Watch your form: Don't pull the weight with your arms or back. Keep your elbows at the same angle so your core muscles control the movement.

HANGING WEIGHTED TWIST

Lower rectus abdominis, obliques, transverse abdominis

Hang from a bar and have a partner place a light medicine ball between your knees.

Rock your pelvis upward, then slowly raise your knees up and to the left. Slowly lower your legs and repeat, this time to the right.

Watch your form: Raising your knees before your pelvis can cause you to engage more of your hip flexors—the muscles along the front of the thighs. Think of the move in two parts: Tilt your pelvis up first, then raise your legs.

V TWIST

Rectus abdominis, obliques

Lie on your back with your knees bent 90 degrees and your feet off the floor so your thighs are perpendicular to the floor. Fold your hands across your chest.

Slowly straighten your legs away from you and to the right. (They should end up at a 45-degree angle to the floor.) As you go, crunch your torso upward and to the left while extending your arms forward. Slowly lower yourself back to the starting position. Repeat the exercise in the other direction.

Watch your form: Spend at least 2 to 3 seconds going up and the same going down. Rushing can disrupt your balance and force you to stop.

BY MYATT MURPHY

Build Bolder Shoulders

Here's how to get shoulders that give you power and an impressive build

The shoulder is not a single muscle. That rounded deltoid covering the joint has three parts, or heads. The anterior head (in front) flexes to move the humerus (upper-arm bone) up and forward and rotate it inward. The posterior head (behind the joint) moves the humerus to the rear and rotates it outward. The medial head (on the side) lifts the arm out to the side and aids the other heads.

Think of shoulders as three smaller muscles. "Most men focus on pressing exercises, which target the anterior and medial heads of the deltoid, but not the posterior head," says Ron Thomson, CSCS, strength and conditioning coach at Purdue University. This can create an imbalance that pulls your shoulder joints out of alignment. The end result: rounded shoulders that appear smaller and interfere with your arms' rotation, increasing your risk of injury. Thomson's workout hits all the heads of the deltoids and "restabilizes your shoulders, pulling them into perfect alignment for more energy, power, and injury protection," he says.

The Payoff

Upper-body strength! Your shoulders help in many exercises that strengthen other muscle groups. For instance, your shoulders assist in many compound moves, including the bench press, incline chest press, bent-over row, and pullup. Having strong shoulders means you can lift more weight in these moves for a better overall body.

An imposing physique! Big shoulders make your waist seem slimmer and give your torso a flared appearance. This V shape conveys power on the field, on the court—and even in the office, though you may have to have your sport coats altered.

Extra power! In any sport, shoulders play a vital role. Whenever you reach, throw, pull, or swing, your arms rotate from the shoulder joints. Strong shoulder muscles help move your arms with more power and speed—and fewer injuries.

Faster feet! Pumping your arms is crucial to sprinting. Your shoulders need to be sturdy and resilient to keep your arms in sync with your feet. Strong shoulder muscles add length to your stride and speed to every step.

The Workout

This routine has four sections. The first, pressing exercises, works two heads of the deltoids simultaneously, as well as the triceps. The remaining three sections hit individual heads—anterior, medial, or posterior—for gains in strength and definition. The classic overhead press can overstress the shoulders when you use heavy weights. This routine incorporates variations of the press to exhaust the shoulder muscles with more intensity and less weight.

It's easy to overwork your shoulders. Use this routine right after training your chest or back, when your shoulders are already partially exhausted. Twice a week is ideal; your shoulders need rest to grow.

HARDTRUTH
Average cost of all medical care and rehabilitation for rotator-cuff surgery:
$50,302

The 4-Week Program

	WEEK 1	WEEK 2	WEEK 3	WEEK 4
Create your routine by . . .	Picking one move from each section (A,B,C,D)	Combining the 4 moves you didn't use in week 1	Doing all 8 moves in the order shown	Doing all 8 moves in the order shown
Sets per exercise:	3	3	2	2
Total number sets per workout:	12	12	16	16
Repetitions per set:	8–12 (except military press)	8–12 (except military press)	8–12 (except military press)	8–12 (except military press)
Speed of each repetition:	2 seconds up, 2 seconds down (except negative press)	2 seconds up, 2 seconds down (except negative press)	2 seconds up, 2 seconds down (except negative press)	2 seconds up, 2 seconds down (except negative press)
Rest between sets:	30 seconds	30 seconds	45 seconds	45 seconds
Do this workout . . .	Twice a week	Twice a week	Twice a week	Twice a week

SECTION A

STANDING MILITARY PRESS

Anterior and medial deltoids, triceps

Using a squat rack and a weight you can lift for eight repetitions, hold the bar with an overhand grip, hands slightly more than shoulder-width apart.

Keeping your back straight and your face forward, slowly press the weight overhead until your arms are fully extended, elbows unlocked. Pause, lower the bar to your chest, and repeat. After eight reps, remove enough weight to allow you to do six to eight repetitions. After that set, strip enough weight to allow six to eight more reps.

Watch your form: Don't rush. Think 2 seconds up, 2 seconds down.

NEGATIVE SHOULDER PRESS

Anterior and medial deltoids, triceps, upper trapezius

Place a bench in front of a squat rack. Use half the weight you can lift 8 to 10 times. Grab the bar with your hands slightly wider than shoulder-width apart and sit on the bench, feet flat on the floor.

Press the bar overhead for a count of three, then take 6 seconds to lower it to the front of your chest.

Watch your form: The slow pace can make you shake and cause the weight to shift forward, which could stress shoulder tendons. Concentrate on lifting and lowering in a straight line.

SECTION B

BARBELL FRONT RAISE

Anterior deltoids

Stand with your feet hip-width apart and hold a light barbell with your hands shoulder-width apart. Your arms should hang straight down, palms facing the front of your thighs.

Keeping your arms straight, slowly lift the bar up and out in front of you until your arms are parallel to the floor. Pause, then slowly lower the bar until your hands barely touch your thighs.

Watch your form: Don't let the bar rest on your thighs after each repetition. You want to keep a little tension on your anterior deltoids and ensure that your shoulders are constantly working.

DUMBBELL FRONT RAISE
Anterior deltoids

Stand with your feet about 12 inches apart and hold a light dumbbell in each hand, arms at your sides, palms toward you.

Keeping your arms straight, slowly raise the weights out in front of you until your arms are parallel to the floor, simultaneously rotating your wrists until your palms face down. Pause, then slowly reverse the movement.

Watch your form: Keep your feet flat. If your heels or toes come off the floor, you're using momentum to raise the weights.

SECTION C

CABLE SINGLE-ARM LATERAL RAISE
Medial deltoids

Stand between the towers of a cable-crossover system with your feet shoulder-width apart. Grab the low-pulley handles (left handle with right hand, right with left) and start with your hands crossed just below your waist.

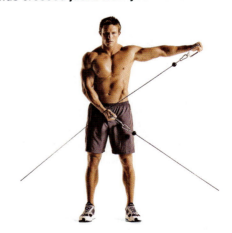

With your elbow slightly bent, slowly raise your left arm out to the side until your arm is parallel to the floor. Pause, slowly reverse the motion, then repeat with your right arm.

Watch your form: Keep your back straight and don't lean back. Do the exercise slowly, 2 seconds up and 2 seconds down.

SEATED LATERAL RAISE
Medial deltoids

Sit on a bench and hold a light dumbbell in each hand, arms at your sides.

Keeping your arms straight and elbows unlocked, slowly sweep your arms out to the sides until they're parallel to the floor and your palms face down. Your upper body should form a T. Pause, then slowly lower your arms to your sides.

Watch your form: Stop just short of touching the bench when you lower your arms, to keep your medial deltoids flexed throughout the exercise.

SECTION D

BENT-OVER CABLE RAISE
Posterior deltoids

Stand between the stacks of a cable station, cross your hands in front of you, and bend down. Grab the left low-pulley handle with your right hand and the right one with your left hand.

With your knees slightly bent and your back straight, bend forward until your back is almost parallel to the floor. Slowly raise your arms out to your sides until they're parallel to the floor. Pause, then slowly lower your arms.

Watch your form: Keep your head and neck in line with your torso. Looking up can work the medial deltoids instead of the posterior deltoids.

The fastest way to big arms is to work your triceps, which account for more than 60 percent of the muscle mass in your upper arms. But most men focus on the biceps, which are easier to see—and to build, says Walt Thompson, PhD, a professor of kinesiology and health at Georgia State University.

Developing arms that aren't just great looking but great lifting requires working every muscle from shoulder to wrist. Sandwiched between the biceps and humerus (the upper-arm bone) is the brachialis. The triceps, on the back of the upper arm, is composed of three muscle groups: the lateral, medial, and long heads. Wrist flexors and extensors lie along the sides of the forearm.

This plan targets all five muscles that make up the biceps and triceps. Barbell and preacher curls ignore the brachialis (which pushes your biceps outward), but this workout hits it. And the triceps moves here will single out the long head, on the inner side of the arm, which is neglected in many other arm workouts.

The Payoff

A stronger grip! Almost every biceps exercise requires a tight grip to hold the weight, so you're indirectly strengthening your forearms and wrists whenever you train your arms. This gives you a stronger grip, perfect for keeping your hands from slipping during moves like deadlifts, shrugs, and upright rows.

More speed! Strong arms make you faster. Your arms help propel you forward and stabilize your body as you swing them. Training your biceps adds power for pumping your arms, so they can keep pace with your legs for a more explosive stride.

Extra power! The three muscle heads that make up the triceps extend the elbow to straighten the arm—necessary for pitching a baseball, shooting a free throw, landing a punch, or pushing a weight off your chest. Stronger triceps mean better performance.

Pain-free shoulders! If your biceps are stronger than your triceps, the imbalance can cause shoulder pain and elbow problems. Equal strength means stable joints and less pain.

The Workout

Perform this routine in its entirety or in sections. Remember that the biceps act as secondary movers in many back exercises, and the triceps assist in many moves that develop the chest and shoulders. So, to completely fatigue your triceps, consider working them on days when you focus on your chest and shoulders. Likewise, throw in some exercises for your biceps and forearms when you work your back.

Train your arms no more than twice a week. Depending on which type of workout schedule you follow, use these arm exercises either at the end of upper-body workouts or on days when you don't work your upper body at all. That way, your arms are never too exhausted to assist larger, stronger muscles earlier in each routine.

The 4-Week Program

	WEEK 1	WEEK 2	WEEK 3	WEEK 4
Create your routine by . . .	Doing exercises 1 and 2 in sections A and B, plus both moves in C	Doing exercises 2 and 3 in sections A and B, plus both moves in C	Doing exercises 1 and 3 in sections A and B, plus both moves in C	Doing all of the moves in section A, then section B, then section C
Sets per exercise:	3	3	3	3
Total number sets per workout:	18	18	18	18
Repetitions per set:	8–12	8–12	8–12	8–12
Speed of each repetition:	2 seconds up, 2 seconds down	2 seconds up, 2 seconds down	2 seconds up, 2 seconds down	2 seconds up, 2 seconds down
Rest between sets:	15 seconds	15 seconds	15 seconds	15 seconds
Do this workout . . .	Twice a week	Twice a week	Twice a week	Twice a week

SECTION A

WALL CURL

Biceps

With your feet and hands shoulder-width apart, stand against a wall and hold a light barbell in front of your thighs. Press your back against the wall so that your head, back, triceps, and heels touch it.

Keeping your elbows close to your body, slowly curl the barbell up until your hands are in front of your shoulders. Squeeze your biceps, then slowly lower the bar.

Watch your form: Performing this move against a wall makes it nearly impossible to cheat. Keep your head, back, and triceps in contact with the wall and avoid letting yourself slide down it.

ALTERNATING-GRIP HAMMER CURL

Biceps, biceps brachialis, forearms

Sit on the edge of a bench and hold a dumbbell in each hand, with your arms hanging at your sides and your palms toward you.

Keeping your back straight, slowly curl the weights up until your thumbs are near your shoulders. Squeeze your biceps, then lower the weights. Next, rotate your wrists inward so your palms face behind you. Slowly curl the weights up, then slowly lower them.

Watch your form: Don't turn your wrists as you curl, as some biceps exercises require you to do. Rotate them only at the end of each repetition.

PAUSE REVERSE CURL

Biceps, biceps brachialis, forearms

Stand holding a light barbell with an overhand grip (palms down).

Keeping your elbows close to your sides, slowly curl the bar up until your forearms are parallel to the floor. Pause for 3 seconds, then continue to curl the bar until it reaches your chest. Slowly lower the bar until your forearms are again parallel to the floor. Pause for another 3 seconds, then lower the bar to the starting position.

Watch your form: Start by using just the bar, with no added weight. Don't cheat by swinging your elbows out and forward. Keep them pointing down at all times.

SECTION B

TWISTING ROPE PULLDOWN
Triceps

Attach a rope handle to a high-pulley cable and grab an end with each hand. Spread your hands about 6 to 8 inches apart. Keeping your upper arms tucked at your sides, pull the rope down until your forearms are parallel to the floor. This is the starting position.

Slowly pull the rope down until your fists reach your thighs, then rotate your wrists so your palms face out, away from your body. Squeeze your triceps for a second, then reverse the move to return to the starting position.

Watch your form: Stare straight ahead. Looking down may cause you to lean forward and let your shoulders assist.

CROSS-SHOULDER EXTENSION
Triceps

Lie on an incline bench and hold a light dumbbell overhead in your right hand, with your palm facing left. Place your left hand on your right triceps for support.

Slowly bend your right arm to lower the weight to your left shoulder, keeping your wrist straight throughout the exercise. (You may need to tilt your head to the right to keep it out of the way.) Raise the weight back overhead and repeat for one set. Switch hands for the next set.

Watch your form: Make sure your upper arm remains stationary as you lower the weight. This keeps stress off your shoulder.

OVERHEAD CABLE TRICEPS EXTENSION

Triceps

Attach a rope handle to a high-pulley cable and grab an end with each hand. Stand with your back to the weight stack, lean forward with one foot ahead of the other, and hold the rope just over your head with your arms bent. (Your upper arms should be almost parallel to the floor.)

Straighten your arms in front of you. Pause, then slowly allow the resistance to pull your hands back overhead.

Watch your form: If your upper arms move up and down, you're using your chest muscles instead of letting your triceps do the work.

SECTION C

WRIST TWIST

Forearms

Stand holding a light dumbbell in each hand with your arms at your sides, palms facing behind you. Bend your arms to curl the weights up until your forearms are parallel to the floor. This is the starting position.

Rotate your wrists until your palms face the ceiling, then rotate them back so your palms face the floor once again. That's one repetition.

Watch your form: Go as slowly as possible. Rushing works less muscle and places tendons at risk of injury.

DOUBLE WRIST CURL

Forearms

Sit on a weight bench with your feet flat on the floor and a 3- or 5-pound dumbbell in each hand. Rest your forearms on your thighs so your wrists hang over your knees and turn your palms down. (You may have to lean forward slightly.)

Bending only at the wrists, lower the dumbbells as far as you can, then raise them as high as possible. Repeat for one set. Next, do the same with your palms facing up.

Watch your form: To keep your biceps from helping, imagine that your forearms are glued to your legs.

BY MYATT MURPHY

Sculpt a Powerful Chest

Strength and size where you want it

There are two approaches to building an impressive chest. "The classic method is to isolate the pectoral muscles and minimize the involvement of other, secondary muscles," says celebrity trainer Steve Lischin, MS, NASM, CPT. "However, a smarter plan for more strength and power begins with teaching your chest, shoulders, triceps, and other upper-body muscles to work together." Compound exercises that involve your upper body and incorporate functional core strength will make that happen. This plan gives you exercises that isolate your chest muscles for size and exercises that integrate your shoulders and triceps for strength.

Your chest is composed of two muscle groups: the pectoralis major and a smaller, deeper group called the pectoralis minor. Changing the angle of your body during classic chest exercises can challenge different parts of these muscle groups for maximum development. The anterior deltoids—the front of the shoulders—and the triceps assist your pectoral muscles. Strengthen them and you can use heavier weights for even more growth.

The Payoff

Impressive power! The bench press is typically—though incorrectly—considered the true measure of a man's strength. A powerful chest will give you an impressive answer to the classic question "Whaddaya bench?" And people will think you must be equally strong in other exercises.

A thinner waistline! Building a bigger, stronger chest also adds size to your shoulders and triceps. The larger you are on top, the smaller your waistline appears.

More fat burning! Swimming burns an astounding 280 to 400 calories in 30 minutes, depending on the stroke—with little risk of injury. Stronger pectoral and shoulder muscles give you more pulling power with every stroke and keep your upper body from tiring out before your legs do, so you can stay in the water for a longer workout.

An edge in sports! A strong chest is a big advantage in sports: setting picks in hoops, pushing off in football. Extra muscle packed onto your upper body also protects you against errant elbows and intentional punches. Build a bigger chest and you'll dominate.

The Workout

You'll start the routine with a bench-press superset: a barbell bench press immediately followed by a dumbbell bench press. (The dumbbell press can be performed on a stability ball to develop core strength.) Then you'll follow with exercises from the other four sections of the workout. This mix places your body in various positions to thoroughly train your middle, upper, lower, inner, and outer pectoral muscles, as well as your shoulders. The workout finishes with a power move for your triceps, the weakest of the muscle groups that contribute to chest strength.

Muscles must rest to grow. Perform the workout twice a week, but listen to your body. If you feel sore, do the routine only once a week.

The 4-Week Program

	WEEK 1	WEEK 2	WEEK 3	WEEK 4
Create your routine by doing the superset, then . . .	Picking one exercise from each section	Picking one exercise from each section (except those chosen in week 1)	Picking one exercise from each section	Doing all the exercises in the routine
Sets per exercise:	3	3	4	4 of the superset; 2 of all the rest
Total number sets per workout:	15	15	20	20
Repetitions per set:	12–15, 8–12, 6–8	12–15, 8–12, 6–8	12–15, 10–12, 8–12, 6–8	Superset: 12–15, 10–12, 8–12, 6–8; remaining exercises: 8–12, 6–8
Speed of each repetition:	2 seconds up, 2 seconds down	2 seconds up, 2 seconds down	2 seconds up, 2 seconds down	2 seconds up, 2 seconds down
Rest between sets:	60–90 seconds	60–90 seconds	90–120 seconds	2 minutes
Do this workout . . .	Twice a week	Twice a week	Once or twice a week	Once or twice a week

BENCH-PRESS SUPERSET

BARBELL BENCH PRESS

Chest, shoulders, triceps

Lie on a bench with your feet flat on the floor. Grab the barbell with an overhand grip (palms facing away from you), your hands slightly more than shoulder-width apart. Remove the bar from the uprights and position it above your chest with your arms straight.

Slowly lower the bar to your chest, just below your nipples. Pause, then press the weight back up until your arms are straight again. After finishing the set, return the bar to the uprights and move to the dumbbell bench press.

Watch your form: Avoid arching your back as you push the weight above your chest, which puts your spine at risk of injury. Instead, press your back into the bench and keep your abs drawn in.

DUMBBELL BENCH PRESS

Chest, shoulders, triceps

Grab a pair of dumbbells and lie back on the bench, positioning the weights along the sides of your chest.

Press the dumbbells straight up, lower them, and repeat for one set.

Watch your form: Avoid arching your back as you push the weight above your chest, which puts your spine at risk of injury. Instead, press your back into the bench and keep your abs drawn in.

SECTION A

SEATED TWISTING CABLE FLY

Inner chest

Sit on a bench between the towers of a cable-crossover station and grab a handle from the bottom of each weight stack. Slide forward on the bench until your arms are extended slightly behind you.

Maintaining a slight bend in your elbows, slowly draw your hands forward until your arms are in front of your chest. As you go, rotate your hands so your palms face out at the top. Pause, then reverse the motion back to the starting position.

Watch your form: Keep your torso upright to avoid unnecessary stress on your lower back.

The 4-Week Program

	WEEK 1	WEEK 2	WEEK 3	WEEK 4
Create your routine by doing the superset, then . . .	Picking one exercise from each section	Picking one exercise from each section	Picking two exercises from each section	Doing all the exercises in both sections in the order shown
Sets per exercise:	2	3	2	1
Total number sets per workout:	4 sets	5 sets	8 sets	8 sets
Repetitions per set:	8–12	8–12	8–12	8–12
Speed of each repetition:	2 seconds up, 2 seconds down	3 seconds up, 3 seconds down	4 seconds up, 4 seconds down	4 seconds up, 4 seconds down
Rest between sets:	45–60 seconds	30–45 seconds	15–30 seconds	None
Do this workout . . .	3 times a week	3 or 4 times a week	4 times a week	5 times a week

SECTION A

STABILITY-BALL CURL UP

Upper abs, obliques

Recline on a stability ball with your head, shoulders, and back in contact with the ball and your feet flat on the floor. Fold your arms across your chest, touching each hand to the opposite shoulder. Pull your belly button in toward your spine to keep your abs tight throughout the move. This helps focus the move more on your abs.

Slowly curl your torso up, vertebra by vertebra, stopping just short of an upright seated position. Then lower yourself to the starting position.

Watch your form: The ball should not move as you curl.

TWISTING MEDICINE-BALL TOSS

Upper abs, obliques

You'll need a partner. Sit on the floor with your hands in front of your chest, knees bent, feet flat on the floor. Your partner should stand a few feet in front of you and to your right.

Have your partner toss a medicine ball toward your right side.

Catch it, then twist your body to your left, lowering your torso as you go. Touch the ball to the floor.

PAINkiller

I've had a slight pain in my lower abdomen for years. It hurts most when I do certain crunches. Is this a lurking hernia?

Tough to call from here. Go to your doctor. An inguinal hernia is a tender bulge in the groin or scrotum that can form suddenly after heavy lifting, severe coughing, straining, or bending. Or one can appear gradually over several weeks. You may experience discomfort that worsens when you bend or lift. Most hernias can't be prevented, but maintaining proper weight and keeping toned might help. The first step is seeking the right diagnosis.

Toss the ball across your body, back to your partner. After a set, reverse the exercise, with your partner throwing the ball from your left.

Watch your form: As you throw the ball, try to keep your arms straight.

STABILITY-BALL CURL UP WITH KNEE TUCK

Upper and lower abs, obliques

Recline on a stability ball, feet flat on the floor, arms crossed on your chest. Your head, shoulders, and back should all be in contact with the ball.

Slowly curl your shoulders and upper back up off the ball as you simultaneously draw your left knee toward your chest. Lower your left leg as you lower your torso back down against the ball. Repeat the motion, this time drawing your right knee toward your chest. Continue alternating legs until you've completed all your repetitions.

Watch your form: Resist the urge to watch your knee move toward your chest.

V RAISE

Upper and lower abs, obliques

Lie on your back with your knees bent at 90 degrees and your feet raised so your thighs are perpendicular to the floor.

Slowly extend your legs so they're at a 45-degree angle from the floor as you raise your upper body so your torso is also at 45 degrees. Extend your arms straight out in front of you.

Pause, then slowly raise your arms up and back over your head until they're in line with your upper body. Lower your arms so they're parallel to the floor, and return to the starting position.

Watch your form: If balancing is difficult, raise your arms only as high as you can.

SECTION B

HANGING REVERSE TRUNK TWIST

Upper and lower abs, obliques

Hang from a pullup bar with your hands shoulder-width apart and your legs slightly bent.

Keeping your legs at this angle, raise them in front of you until your thighs are parallel to the floor.

Next, tilt your pelvis and slowly raise your legs until your feet are almost as high as your chest.

Lower your legs to the middle position and rotate them to the right (so your feet point to 1 o'clock), then to the left (feet pointing to 11 o'clock). Bring your legs back to the center, then to the starting position.

Watch your form: Think about tilting your pelvis up, then lifting your legs.

SINGLE-RESISTANCE DOUBLE CRUNCH

Upper and lower abs

Attach a bar to a low-pulley cable. Sit facing the pulley. Place the cable between your feet so that the bar rests across your insteps. Rest your head and back flat on the floor, bend your knees at a 90-degree angle, and position your thighs perpendicular to the floor.

Keeping your legs at a 90-degree angle, slowly curl your head and shoulders off the floor as you tilt your pelvis and curl your legs toward your chest. Pause, then return to the starting position.

Watch your form: Try to curl your lower body forward to roll your butt off the floor.

V RAISE/KNEE TUCK

Upper and lower abs, transverse abdominis

Lie faceup on the floor with your knees bent at 90 degrees and your feet raised so your thighs are perpendicular to the floor.

Slowly extend your legs so they're at a 45-degree angle from the floor and simul-

taneously raise your upper body so your torso is also at 45 degrees.

Extend your arms straight out in front of you. Holding this position, slowly draw your left

knee in to your chest, then extend it back out. Repeat the motion with your right leg. Continue to alternate legs.

Watch your form: Go slowly. Imagine that each foot is resisting something heavy.

DOUBLE-RESISTANCE DOUBLE CRUNCH

Upper and lower abs

Attach a rope to one of the low-pulley cables and a bar to the other low cable. Lie flat on your back with your head pointing toward the rope and your feet toward the bar. Place the bar on the tops of your shoes so the cable is between your feet. Reach back, grab both ends of the rope, and pull your fists to your chest.

Slowly curl your torso up as you simultaneously tilt your pelvis and curl your legs toward your chest. Hold for a second, then slowly lower yourself.

Watch your form: Try to resist the urge to pull the rope with your arms.

Burn Off Your Belly

BY MIKE MEJIA, MS, CSCS

Guard against holiday weight gain with this batch of fat-burning exercises. This routine challenges your largest muscle groups to burn calories and stokes your metabolism. Perform these exercises as a circuit, moving from one to the next without rest. Do two or three circuits, resting 60 seconds after each. Do this routine 3 days a week and rest a day between sessions.

Dumbbell clean and press: Stand with your knees slightly bent and hold a pair of dumbbells at knee level.

Keeping your chest up and your back arched, straighten yourself in an explosive movement, pulling the weights to chest height.

Continue to rise onto the balls of your feet, then quickly drop underneath the weights and "catch" them on your shoulders with your elbows high.

Press the weights overhead, then lower them and return to the starting position. Do 6 to 8 repetitions.

T pushup: Hold a light pair of dumbbells with your palms facing each other, and get into the down position of a pushup.

Perform a basic pushup. At the top, lift one dumbbell toward the ceiling while rotating your torso in the same direction so you face to the side. (Your body should resemble the letter T.) Return to the starting position and repeat, this time lifting the opposite arm. Do 8 to 10 reps.

Reverse lunge and curl: Stand holding a pair of dumbbells at arm's length.

Take a step backward as you bend your knee until it forms a 90-degree angle at the bottom. As you step back, curl the weights to your shoulders. Lower them as you push yourself back to the starting position. Repeat the move, this time lunging with your other leg. Do 6 to 8 reps with each leg.

Seated dumbell rotation: Sit on the floor with your knees bent and hold a dumbbell at its ends, in front of your chest. Lift your feet off the floor and cross your ankles so you balance on your butt while leaning back slightly.

Next, rapidly rotate from side to side as you attempt to touch the weight to the floor. Do 8 to 10 rotations in each direction.

Training
Tips

Does it matter what size stability ball I use for crunches?

The perfect fit should allow your entire torso to be supported and in full contact with the ball at the bottom of the crunch. Your thighs should be about parallel to the floor. But comfort's important, too.

A larger ball has a gradual arch, so you'll feel less of a stretch in your abdominals, while the more abrupt arch of a smaller ball puts your body in a more pronounced stretch position. As your flexibility improves, drop to a smaller size.

My shoulders pop when I lift weights, no matter how much weight I use. Should I be worried?

It's like clicking in the knee or elbow; in most cases, nothing's wrong. The sound is likely caused by soft-tissue movement or improper displacement of the limbs at the elbow joint. You should have a trainer check your form, and if you feel pain or find that your range of motion is limited, stop and consult a physician.

I read that you can work your abs every day with crunches, but I'm getting nowhere. Am I doing something wrong?

Muscles responsible for maintaining an upright posture (such as your deep abdominal stabilizers) are used to working all the time. But many ab exercises, like the crunch, neglect these muscles and stress the rectus abdominis, a muscle that needs time to recover. Crunching every day overtrains your abs. Try the plank instead. It challenges your postural muscles, so you can perform it frequently—even every day—for a stronger core.

The plank: Get into a modified pushup position with your forearms on the floor. Keep your abs tight and your body straight for 60 seconds.

I use resistance bands to strengthen my rotator cuffs, and it seems to be working. Can I use bands for larger muscle groups?

Absolutely. Bands are simple to use and easy to pack for on-the-road workouts. You may need a

thicker band than you've been using for your rotator cuffs, so that it provides enough resistance to challenge your larger muscle groups. The downside of bands is that exercises tend to be very easy at the beginning of the motion and hard at the end, because resistance increases as the band stretches. Continue using other forms of resistance as well, such as free weights and cables.

How can I build my chest without aggravating my oft-injured shoulders?

Let's create a long-term, pain-free solution by getting your shoulders healthy instead. The chest is part of the shoulders, so you can't build one without the other. See a qualified physical therapist who specializes in sports and ask for a program that will open up your chest muscles, strengthen your upper back, and allow you to elevate your sternum so your shoulders fall into proper alignment. Then you can strengthen your rotator-cuff and scapular muscles and begin a balanced training plan. The idea is to build a great-looking, pain-free body for life—not just for the next 6 months, until you need shoulder surgery.

My pecs flatten out in the middle of my chest. How do I get that full-chest look?

There are no magic exercises that target the inner part of the pectoral muscles. But you can still develop a better-looking chest by improving the flexibility of your pecs and latissimus dorsi—the fan-shaped muscles of your back. "Too much pec and lat work—such as bench presses and lat pulldowns—can cause these muscles to shorten, pulling your shoulders forward and in toward each other," says personal trainer Mike Mejia, MS, CSCS. This can make the outer chest appear more developed than the muscle fibers closer to the midline of your body.

Stretch your chest and back and add the reverse pushup to your workout. It strengthens the muscles that pull back your shoulder blades, which in turn improves the appearance of your inner pecs.

Reverse pushup: Lie under a barbell set in the supports of a squat rack. Grab the bar with your thumbs on the same side of the bar as your fingers and support your weight on the backs of your heels. Pull yourself up until your chest almost touches the bar. Hold this position for 3 seconds, then slowly lower yourself until your arms are straight. Do two or three sets of 6 to 10 reps.

Some guys work the same muscle group with different exercises on consecutive days. Is it possible to recover that fast?

Just because your body can handle something—binge drinking, for example—doesn't mean you should do it. Targeting the same muscle group every day sets you up for injury because you're ignoring some muscles while overtraining others. Muscles grow best if you give them ample time to recover. Wait 48 to 72 hours to work a muscle group again. You'll be able to put in more effort for better results.

RUN
FAST

How can something so simple—left right, left right, repeat over and over and over—be so complex: training schedules, workout plans, $159 running shoes?

We think it's because like anything else in life, what you put into running determines what you get out of it. And the rewards are huge. Running is scientifically proven to keep your heart healthy, and now it's been shown to improve your brainpower, too. We may be so bold as to say that running can reduce your risk of nearly every known disease.

That's powerful motivation. And whether you're running away from disease, after your kids, or toward a finish line, this chapter offers advice for you. You'll learn how to shave minutes off of your race time. Then you'll discover the importance of hill training to increase your speed and improve your body. You'll also read about one runner's experience at Grand Targhee Resort for the Badwater Ultramarathon Training Camp. You can apply the lessons he learned about motivation— for one of the most challenging of sports—to any type of running—or any sport, really.

So lace up those running shoes; here's how to be faster on your feet.

BY ADAM CAMPBELL

Run for Your Life

New science has linked aerobic exercise not just to healthier hearts but to improved brainpower, too. The world's most wildly successful men engage in intense aerobic workouts. Why don't you?

We can make you smarter in 30 minutes.

Not the kind of smart that's acquired through learning something new, like small-engine repair or quadratic equations. We're talking about improving your brain from the inside out, the kind of smart that leads to faster and more accurate decision-making, yields greater productivity, and inspires innovation. If you want to be calculating about it, it's the kind of smart that makes you money.

And all you'll need to invest is a half hour, three or four hundred calories, and 80 bucks for a decent pair of running shoes.

For years, aerobic exercise has been touted for its many health benefits; it's no leap to suggest that it can reduce your risk of nearly every known disease. And this is especially true concerning heart health. But the effect of cardio reaches far beyond lipid profiles and blood-pressure readings. In fact, it may do as much for your brain as it does for your ticker; maybe more.

Richard Haig believes it. When he retired early from his position as president of one of the largest security firms on the East Coast, Haig was financially set for life. At 38, he focused on getting his handicap down to 10 but found that he was crushingly bored. So he took up a new challenge: cardio. What started as a daily 2-mile walk became an ultraendurance lifestyle within a year; he once ran 63 miles nonstop in a charity race. Sure, his fitness level improved, but what he really noticed was that his brain was overflowing. That's when he went back to work.

I know you're supposed to avoid pavement when running, but I'm worried that my knees will get too coddled if I always run on grass. Is there a happy medium?

Coddled? How old-fashioned! The short answer is no—putting in most of your miles on grass doesn't create sissy knees that can't take pavement. Likewise, pavement doesn't toughen them up. Generally speaking, when you have a softer option, use it. Paved roads and sidewalks can be rough on the joints, though you may not notice the damage for years to come. So mix it up. Occasionally running on grass and other soft surfaces (such as a treadmill) will give your knees some relief.

Since Haig's return as CEO, his company, Haig Security Systems, has been as invigorated by his exercise as his body has. "It's no coincidence that I've done more to increase the company's value in the past 2 years than I had in the previous 10," he says.

It's not hard to find successful men who will swear by the effect cardiovascular exercise has had on their careers and their whole lives. But what may surprise you is the number who credit it not just as a component of their success but as the catalyst.

For a group of road-hardened examples, look to the competitors in the CEO Challenge, a program for CEOs competing in Ironman triathlons, which require participants to complete a 2.4-mile swim, a 26.2-mile run, and a 112-mile bike ride in less than 17 hours. At stake: the title "World's Fittest CEO." According to Ted Kennedy (not the senator), president of CEO Challenge, the Colorado company that started the competition 4 years ago, the majority of these executives believe their training

improves all aspects of their lives, from the family dining room to the corporate boardroom. "Most of the men who compete in this event say that without aerobic exercise, they wouldn't be CEOs," he says.

You might consider men like Haig and the Ironman CEOs to be a self-selected group: executives who love to run, cycle, or swim and therefore attribute their success to it. For every successful man who exercises, there are probably two successful men who amply fill—and overflow—the seat of power. No amount of cardio will lead a career hamburger-flipper to invent the next Google, but we propose that in man-to-man competition—fittest versus fattest—cardio does grant an earned, unfair advantage. Call it the aristocracy of cardio. And, according to a growing body of scientific research, it all starts between the ears.

There have been thousands of studies on how aerobic exercise affects cardiovascular health, but there are equally powerful ones that assess its impact on mental performance. Of course, intuitively, one could argue that cardio is just mentally arousing, like a Starbucks double latte. Exercise, after all, raises your heart rate and increases the flow of oxygen-rich blood throughout your body, including your brain. This is a partial explanation, but the whole picture is more complicated.

One of the first studies to find that exercise improves brain performance was a 1986 investigation of 30 women at Purdue University. During the study, the women boosted their fitness levels by 17 percent and simultaneously netted a 12 to 68 percent improvement in their ability to process information and make sound decisions. This suggested, for the first time in a laboratory setting, that exercise improves high-level cognitive function. The women in the study weren't simply more alert; they were, in effect, better thinkers.

In 1991, a Kent State researcher named Wojtek Chodzko-Zajko proposed that the more complex the mental task, the more beneficial the effect of aerobic exercise. Over the next few years, his theory gained currency, and a name was given to the thought process he described. Appropriately enough, it became known as executive control.

Twelve years later, scientists demonstrated the effect of a single session of exercise on these higher mental processes. In his lab at the University of Illinois at Urbana-Champaign, Charles Hillman, PhD, tested the hypothesis that cardio improves a person's ability to process information immediately after exercise. He recruited 20 college-age men and women to work out at a moderate intensity on a treadmill for 30 minutes on two separate occasions. He outfitted them with an electroencephalograph—which looks like a 1920s leather football helmet decorated with two dozen electrodes—allowing him to monitor which brain functions exercise affected most.

At one session, the participants were asked to take a mental test before they exercised; at the other, they took the test afterward. When they worked out before the

The Busy Man's Day Expander

3 ways to make time for cardio

Remember this number: 1.4. That's the percentage of your week that five 30-minute cardio sessions requires, enough for a brain-boosting dose of exercise Monday through Friday. Sound doable? It is.

We talked to dozens of successful, time-crunched men who are dedicated exercisers. Their strategies:

Wake up early. "Once you form the habit, it just becomes ingrained in your lifestyle," says Joe Hogan, CEO of GE Healthcare. He's been waking up at 5 a.m. for 30 minutes of cardio, 4 days a week, for 20 years. A 2005 study published in Health Psychology reports that it took new exercisers about 5 weeks to make their sessions a habit. And hitting the road at dawn doesn't mean you'll miss out on sleep. Researchers at Northwestern University found that men who started exercising in the morning slept better than they had before they began working out.

Prioritize your life. Calculate the average time you spend daily doing everything from analyzing spreadsheets to watching TV. "Once I counted up the wasted hours, it was easy to see that I could fit exercise in by deciding what's most important," says Joe Blesse, a pilot for Continental Express who lost 150 pounds after initiating a cardio program 2 years ago. Blesse's advice: Always give priority to activities that serve the greatest purpose— those involving work, family, and exercise. For example, a 30-minute run trumps a 30-minute sitcom—every time. It's that simple.

Call it multitasking. "I work on my most challenging business issues while running, cycling, or skiing," says David Varwig, CEO of the Citadel Group, a global investment firm. Exercise isn't work time lost; it's an opportunity to focus on problems without distraction. At home, exercising with your spouse or kids is quality time. "Whether it's a hike with my wife or hitting the streets with the baby jogger, I make exercise a family event whenever possible," says David Daggett, an Ironman triathlete and a managing partner at Lewis and Daggett, a North Carolina law firm.

test, they showed increased activity in areas of the brain that control attention and memory. According to Dr. Hillman, this should translate into being able to multitask at a greater speed while making more accurate decisions. Does that sound like a guy fit for the boss's chair, or what?

The results of the electroencephalograph may explain the difference in brain activity. The data showed that the single 30-minute bout of cardio had two major effects on an electrical system of the brain called P3. First, the exercise session "decreased P3 latency," which means subjects were able to process information faster. Second, Dr. Hillman found that the cardio session "increased P3 amplitude," a measurement of brain activity related to memory and focus. So their aerobic exercise helped them concentrate better and recall information faster.

A follow-up study in 2004 yielded similar results, although this time, Dr. Hillman used both younger and older adults. The study found that 60- to 70-year-olds have worse memory and attention spans than 20-year-olds and are slower at processing information. No surprise there. But, just as in the earlier research, older adults who regularly exercised showed faster reaction times and better accuracy than the sedentary seniors.

So, if you're keeping score, hard science shows that running for 30 minutes three times a week leads to an improvement in decision-making proficiency, better memory, a longer attention span, and greater mental longevity. Yet it's arguable that data collected in milliseconds with a sci-fi skullcap don't necessarily manifest themselves in the real-world mental tasks you perform at your job.

But one guy isn't buying that. "I work out solutions to complex problems when I train and put them into action as soon as I get back to the office," says Brian Carroll, president and chief operating officer of Carroll Enterprises, a Boston brokerage firm that provides management services to HMOs, insurance companies, and national banks.

He discovered cardio 3 years ago. "I was 39 and didn't like what I saw in the mirror," he says. He was inspired by the memory of his older brother, who died 4 years earlier of a cardiac condition at 38 and had once challenged Carroll to run the Boston Marathon before he turned 40. At the time, Carroll was 25 pounds overweight and living a high-stress life with three young children.

But he persevered, and 3 weeks before turning 40, he finished the race.

"Cardio brought on a new lifestyle that I find contagious in my life and my business," Carroll says. He's now a veteran of 14 marathons, all while keeping a hectic work schedule of sales meetings, conference calls, and travel. He refuses to do business on the golf course, instead using that time for exercise. "I feel that the heightened mental focus I get from triathlon and marathon training helps me win more deals than I could playing golf," he says.

There is additional lab-based support for the notion that more cardio in your life means more success in the office. Researchers at Leeds Metropolitan University in the United Kingdom recently released findings of a new study that looked at how exercise affects job performance. It worked like this: They asked 210 workers to provide feedback on their job-related duties and time management—first on a day when they participated in an exercise program and again on a day when they did no exercise. They simply reported observations of their own behavior based on a 7-point scale. For example, they were asked to rate their ability to work without stopping for unscheduled breaks and how effectively they were able to stick to their to-do lists. They also provided details about their workloads and exercise sessions. When the results were tallied, even the researchers were surprised.

Workers scored 15 percent higher in their ability to meet both time and output demands on the day they exercised. "What we found staggered us, and we were left

wondering what companies might do otherwise to produce these 15 percent improvements," says Jim McKenna, PhD, the lead researcher.

Consider for a moment what these numbers mean to you: On days when you exercise, you can—theoretically, at least—accomplish in an 8-hour day what normally would take you 9 hours and 25 minutes. Or you'd still work 9 hours but get more done, leaving you feeling less stressed and happier with your job, another perk that the workers reported. Obviously, the responses that led to these results were subjective. But it's hard to deny that perception is reality when it comes to job satisfaction. And a 15 percent

boost in productivity might just give you a case for a similar boost in pay.

Besides showing how Dr. Hillman's laboratory findings are expressed in the real world, this study may explain why busy men who regularly exercise are able to fit cardio into their schedules, while equally busy men who don't exercise claim they don't have the time. Arkansas governor Mike Huckabee can relate to both sides of the story. In June 2003, he was sedentary and weighed 280 pounds; he now runs marathons and weighs 170. "I've never found time to exercise," he says. "I make time."

Consider him a poster boy for what cardio can do for a man who's already good at his job. Huckabee, ever the conscientious politician, wants to be clear: He didn't have a problem keeping his schedule or accomplishing tasks before he started running. And it's true; this guy became governor in 1996—7 years before he initiated his exercise program—and was reelected twice along the way. It's just that he's even better now. "I'm more creative because I have mental energy. When I finish running several miles, it's like my mind is running on overdrive," he says.

"It's made a dramatic difference in my ability to focus."

Focus. It's a word that comes up frequently when you speak with cardio fanatics. It makes sense, given what scientists have already established about the effects of aerobic workouts on mental performance. But focus is really more descriptive of mental state. And in that capacity, cardio appears therapeutic. "Aerobic exercise seems to have a focusing effect similar to that of attention

The Success Workout

Get the edge with the thinking man's exercise plan

The research is clear: Thirty minutes of exercise makes you smarter—immediately. But what about the effects of 20 minutes, or even 10? Scientists don't know yet. So play it safe, and use the same exercise program they used in the lab. Here's all you need to know.

Keep moving for 30 minutes. Any cardio exercise will do—running, cycling, swimming, rowing. In fact, it's best to diversify, especially if you're a beginner, to avoid overuse injuries.

Do your cardio anytime you want a mental boost. For the long haul, doing as few as three sessions a week has been

shown to improve the mental performance of older adults, says Charles Hillman, PhD. So consider that your minimum.

Consider intensity. Even walking appears to have brain benefits, but you need to pick up the pace to ensure that you replicate the results from Dr. Hillman's research. Simply use the Borg Scale, right (named after the Swedish scientist who invented it), to gauge your effort level. It starts at 6, because the numbers correlate very accurately to heart rate when you multiply them by 10. To match the research,

exercise between levels 13 (somewhat hard) and 15 (hard) for the duration of your session. It's a "perceived exertion" scale, so you can't mess up: Just use your own judgment.

The Borg Scale

Exhaustion (you're done) **20**
Extremely hard (fastest you can go) **19**
Very hard (strenuous pace that's hard to maintain) **17**
Hard (about 80 percent of your full effort) **15**
13 Somewhat hard (tiring but steady pace)
11 Fairly light (brisk walking or easy jogging)
9 Very light (easy, slow walking)
6 Resting (sitting on the couch)

deficit disorder medications," says Alex Giorgio, a psychotherapist and founder of a personal consulting group.

Over a span of 15 years, Giorgio worked with more than 10,000 successful people, and by his estimate, 60 percent of them were looking for help with attention difficulties. But there were two subsets in the group: Some had smooth career trajectories; others went through wrenching peaks and valleys. After thousands of interviews with clients, Giorgio identified certain factors that typified smoother career paths. Among the most important: adherence to an aerobic exercise program. The cause could be simple: Like Ritalin, exercise increases blood dopamine levels, upping the rate of communication between different areas of your brain. And when your brain is working better, so are you.

Edward Hallowell, MD, a Harvard-trained psychiatrist and coauthor of *Delivered from Distraction*, concurs with Giorgio's observations. "Cardio is one of the best treatments for ADD and poor mental focus, as well as for anxiety," he says. "It's like a wonder drug for the brain."

And shall we add "happiness" to the list, too? Duke University researchers found that performing moderate-intensity cardio workout three times a week is as effective as the antidepressant Zoloft at reducing major depression. You can't beat that, even if your insurance carrier only requires a co-pay.

Clearly, there are two kinds of men: Those who do cardio and those who don't; the beneficiaries and the men who leave this advantage unclaimed. But if you understand the science—and look at the living, dominant examples of men who embody it—you have to conclude that cardio gives you an edge. In the first 30 minutes, it can make you a better man. If you stick with it, the effects not only last a lifetime but may even extend it.

Think of it as building sweat equity in yourself. It's truly a no-brainer.

BY MATT FITZGERALD

Step on It

Shave minutes off your race times—and pounds off your middle—with these simple tweaks

Men have been running since we shared disputed turf with saber-toothed cats. So how come so many of us do it wrong? Plenty of reasons: desk jobs, cars, couches, complacency. The urgency is lacking; the muscles are unused. Few of us have ever felt the need for a lesson.

Prepare to learn—and burn. Running incinerates fat like nothing else. And a few tweaks to your technique will have you running faster and longer than any of your distant ancestors.

With all the glory available to world-class runners now, it's no surprise that innovative coaches, sports scientists, and runners themselves search for new techniques to grab an edge.

Take Meb Keflezighi, the American who won the silver medal in the marathon at the Athens Olympics. He does things—cross-training, plyometrics, bicycling—that the great American marathoner of the '70s, Bill Rodgers, never considered. (And Meb probably wouldn't consider eating Bill's favorite food, pizza with mayo.) The same cutting-edge methods that hone the likes of Keflezighi can help you. It's time to reject conventional wisdom (CW) and hit the road with newfound wisdom and vigor.

Old CW: You were born with your stride

New CW: Change your stride for the better.

Elite runners move more efficiently than the rest of us, using less energy at any speed. An efficient stride is comfortable and reduces risk of injury. Until recently, running coaches and biomechanics experts believed that individual stride patterns were too hardwired for average runners to learn to run more like the elites.

The latest science shows that, with a little patience and discipline, anyone can change his stride for the better. But do it gradually, one modification at a time, and practice each single change with every step until it becomes automatic. Here are the three best efficiency-boosting stride changes you can make.

1. Shorten it. About 8 in 10 recreational runners overstride, according to Alan Hreljac, PhD, a professor of biomechanics at California State University at Sacramento. This creates a thudding, braking effect. To correct it, lean your entire body slightly forward. Your feet will land a little closer to your body.

2. Defy gravity. Reduce the amount of time each foot is on the ground. While you run, think about pulling your leg backward just as your foot makes contact with the ground. A typical plodder lands, stands, and then thrusts backward.

3. Bounce less. Imagine a low ceiling 2 inches above your head. It'll keep your gait smooth and efficient. You don't want up and down; you want forward.

Old CW: Speed is for sprinters

New CW: Speed training helps everyone.

Think back on your past week of running. How much of it was at a brisk, saber-

Gait Keepers

6 keys to efficient running

Run tall. Gravity and weak core muscles cause many runners to "fold" in the middle when their feet land. This sitting-down movement wastes energy. Imagine that wires are attached to your shoulders, pulling you up slightly. Thrust your hips forward a bit and think "stability" when your foot hits. It's easier to run tall if you've worked your core properly; find core exercises at www.menshealth.com/cardio.

Relax. Tension in your arms, shoulders, neck, and face reduces efficiency. Arms and fingers should be loose.

Unclench your hands and let your jaw jiggle.

Breathe right. Your breathing should be rhythmic and deep, and you should feel your diaphragm, not your chest, doing the work. Exhale with controlled force. When you pick up the pace, don't let your breathing get shallow.

Land on the midfoot. A heel-first landing is a brake. It means you're extending your leg out too far in front of your center of gravity, so it takes more energy to move forward. And it's shaky, so your muscles are working on stabilization instead of forward motion. Shorten your stride. It'll feel

odd at first, like shuffling, but once you get used to it, focus on thrusting backward with force.

Run softly. The louder your footfalls, the less efficiently you're running. Try running more quietly; you'll be unconsciously switching to a midfoot strike and a shorter, quicker stride.

Swing symmetrically. Check your form on a treadmill in front of a mirror. If one arm is bent more than the other or swings more, you have a musculoskeletal imbalance that can slow you down. Target the weaker side with strength and flexibility exercises.

---

tooth-eluding clip? Today's top runners do as much as 20 percent of their training at speeds faster than race pace. This conditions the fast-twitch muscle fibers that are seldom recruited during slower running. It also maximizes aerobic capacity (the rate at which your muscles use oxygen) and increases stride power and efficiency.

Speed training also makes you ripped. You burn more calories because, simply, it takes more energy to run hard. And fast running is the perfect companion to strength training—both work the fast-twitch muscle fibers. Here's a speed-training format to try.

The ladder: Do this workout at a running track.

1. Warm up with 5 to 10 minutes of easy jogging, followed by stretches for the hamstrings and calves.

2. Run one lap hard, then jog one lap.

3. Run two laps hard and jog one.

4. Run three laps hard and jog one.

5. Optional: Run four laps hard.

6. Cool down with 5 to 10 minutes of easy jogging.

Old CW: Run up hills, then jog back down

New CW: Run down hills, then jog back up.

Downhill running is integral to the training of elite distance runners. Running downhill increases stress on your legs, which makes them better able to handle impact—as long as you don't overdo it. Running downhill can help you go faster, because your muscles will grow accustomed to the quicker stride required.

Once or twice a week, after completing an easy run, do four to six relaxed downhill sprints (not on a steep hill, just an easy grade) lasting about 20 seconds apiece.

Recover between sprints by jogging slowly back up the hill.

Old CW: Strength makes you faster

New CW: Explosive power makes you faster.

You know by now that cross-training helps your running by strengthening the rest of your body while giving your running muscles and joints a break. Next step: Add plyometrics, or jumping drills. You'll improve your efficiency and power.

Researchers at the University of Jyväskylä in Finland found that runners who replaced a third of their weekly running with plyometrics improved their 5-K race times by roughly 3 percent, while a control group saw no improvement. So if you run a 25-minute 5-K, you can shave a minute off your time by running less. Try these plyometric exercises.

Split squat leap: Stand with your left foot half a step ahead of your right foot, your hands at your sides. Lower yourself until your back knee is about an inch off the floor, then leap as high off the floor as you can. (Drive your arms up above you to help propel your body upward.) While airborne, reverse the position of your feet so that when you land, your right foot is a half step ahead of your left. Immediately lower yourself into another deep squat. Complete 16 to 24 jumps (8 to 12 in each position).

Single-leg box jump: Balance on your left foot facing a sturdy platform (such as an exercise step) that's 10 to 18 inches high. Leap onto the platform, landing on your left foot, and immediately jump back down to the floor on the same foot. Do 10 to 20 repetitions, then switch to your right foot and repeat.

Old CW: Make every run count

New CW: Use the "hard-easy" rule.

Use a 1-to-10 scale to rate how challenging your workouts are. Most runners hover around a 5 (not hard, not easy) day after day after day. Today's top runners avoid this gray zone by doing runs that are either truly challenging (8 and above) or very easy (3 and below).

The reason? The biggest fitness gains come from the hardest workouts, but you can't take yourself to the limit every time you lace up your Asics. Follow the hard-easy rule, and you can achieve better results with the same total amount of training you're doing now. You'll be able to push harder on some days by allowing your body to recover on others. This will help you avoid overtraining, and you won't tire from a repetitive routine.

Let's say you run four times a week at level 5. This week, try doing two level-8 runs (one long run and one speed session) and two level 2s (short, easy runs). Either approach adds up to 20 effort "points." Stick with the hard-easy schedule for a couple of months and check your race times. Your numbers should be smaller.

Old CW: Stick to your plan

New CW: Free your mind, man.

Too many runners treat their training plans as gospel. But a growing number are learning the benefits of "training opportunistically." Here's how it works.

You need to do your most challenging runs on days when you feel good. But you never know how you're going to feel until you start running. Forcing yourself to crank out hard runs on predetermined days means you'll inevitably turn in some subpar performances and won't benefit as much as you could.

Begin each workout day with the option of either a Plan A (challenging) or a Plan B (easy) run. If you're headed out for a Plan A effort but feel flat during your warmup, switch to Plan B: an easy run. And if you find you have plenty in the tank on a B day, gear up to an A. Of course, the catch is the temptation to declare all days Plan Bs. Make the switch only if you feel truly lousy. Otherwise, grind through it.

This takes a little discipline. And that's one bit of conventional wisdom that will never change.

PAINkiller

When I run on a treadmill or use a cross-trainer, my toes start tingling, then I lose sensation in my feet. Should I be worried?

Yes, you should start worrying. There might be a problem with your nerves or blood flow, so see a doctor. But first check your shoes. If they're too small or tied too tightly, they may be the cause of the tingling and numbness.

BY DAVID SCHIPPER

Head for the Hills

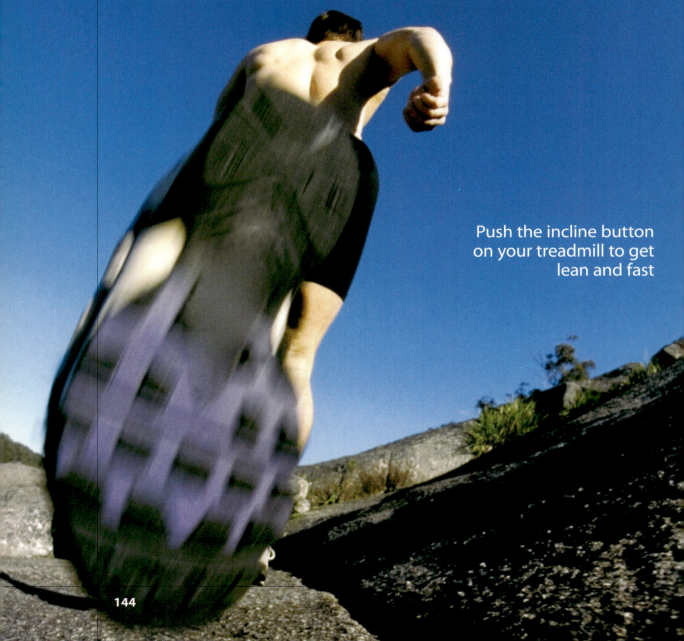

Push the incline button on your treadmill to get lean and fast

You may not know it, but every treadmill comes factory equipped with a "faster results" button. Push it and you'll burn more fat, build stronger legs, and boost your fitness level to an all-time high—without adding a second to your workout. There's just one problem: This magical interface is labeled "incline" on the control panel. And that means hardly anyone touches it.

It's easy to understand why: Running on a grade is harder, even though your pace is slower than on a flat surface. But that extra effort is the driving force of a more efficient workout. Researchers at the University of Georgia found that uphill running activates 9 percent more muscle each stride, compared with exercising at the same relative intensity on level ground.

And if you're not dialing up the incline, you're practically running downhill: English scientists determined that a 1 percent treadmill elevation is needed just to replicate the energy requirements of running on an outdoor track.

Of course, that hill up the road can accomplish the same thing. Feel free to attack it—just follow our advice on page 147. Hills deliver an exhilarating workout and great results for racers, from a personal record in your weekend 5-K to Meb Keflezighi's silver medal in the Athens Olympic Marathon, which came after he added extra hill work to his training.

Either way, moving your workout to higher ground yields greater dividends from the same time investment. Because you can control the degree of incline, treadmills provide an added benefit beyond protection from the elements. "Exercising on a machine allows you to structure hill work that is very specific to your goals and level of fitness," says Rick Morris, author of *Treadmill Training for Runners.*

Ramp up your workout and tap the full potential of your treadmill with our guide to indoor hill training. It's as easy as pushing a button.

The Workouts

Choose the workout that best fits your goals, or rotate workouts. Varying your approach each session is a great way to reap the benefits of each type of training while banishing boredom. Before each workout, warm up for 5 to 10 minutes by walking or jogging at an easy pace.

THE GUT BUSTER

Your goal: Fat loss

Carrying extra pounds makes running harder and increases your risk of overuse injuries, particularly to the knees. But a study in *Medicine & Science in Sports & Exercise* found that an uphill grade of just 3 degrees reduces leg shock by 24 percent. That's why this workout from *Men's Health* contributing editor Michael Mejia, MS, CSCS, intensifies by incline, not speed. "It not only eases the stress on your knees but also increases the involvement of your hips and hamstrings, which quickly elevates heart rate and calorie burn," says Mejia.

Warm up, then increase the belt speed to

4 mph for 3 minutes. That's enough for a fast walk. (Most people don't need to break into a run on a flat surface until at least 4.5 mph.) Maintain that speed for the duration of the workout and simply adjust the incline according to the chart below. You'll notice that the session grows more difficult as you progress, so be prepared to push harder as you go.

If it's too hard: Lower the grade to 0 percent for each 2-minute segment, while keeping the 1-minute intervals as shown in the chart.

TIME	GRADE
1 minute	2%
2 minutes	0%
1 minute	4%
2 minutes	2%
1 minute	6%
2 minutes	4%
1 minute	8%
2 minutes	6%

If it's too easy: Set your speed to 4.5 mph for the duration or simply continue the wave-like progression as long as possible. (So your next step would be a 10 percent grade for 1 minute, followed by an 8 percent grade for 2 minutes.)

THE CHAMPION BUILDER

Your goal: Maximum endurance Swedish researchers found that mara-thoners who ran hills for 12 weeks improved their running economy by 3 percent. This translates to a 2-minute reduction in your 10-mile time and 6 minutes off a marathon—without exerting any more effort in the race. To put that in perspective, consider that 6 minutes was the difference between a medal and 26th place in the 2004 Olympic Marathon. For you, it might mean breaking 4 hours in your first marathon or setting a personal best in your next 10-K.

"This workout features steep, gradual, and rolling hills, bringing all the aspects of hill training into one session," says Morris. You'll be able to recover energy on the short hills in order to charge the long climbs. Set the treadmill to a speed that's about 90 seconds slower than your normal mile pace. So if you usually run 8-minute miles (7.5 mph), set the treadmill to 6.3 mph, the speed equivalent of a 9-minute mile. Then change the incline of the treadmill at the indicated mile marker.

MILE MARKER	INCLINE
0 to 1	1%
1 to 2	2%
2 to 2.5	5%
2.5 to 3	2%
3 to 3.5	8%
3.5 to 4	2%
4 to 4.5	5%
4.5 to 5	2%

If it's too hard: Stop when you've had enough and progress by trying to run 10 seconds longer in your next workout.

If it's too easy: Repeat as many segments as you can, starting at the first mile marker.

THE MOUNTAIN CHALLENGE

Your goal: Sports conditioning

Over the years, professional athletes have used hill training to prepare. And no venue is better known than "the Hill"—a steep 5-mile trail in San Carlos, California's Edgewood Park. It was the site of the legendary off-season training program of former San Francisco 49er and Oakland Raider Jerry Rice for more than 20 years. The rigors of the perpetual ascent simultaneously improve physical conditioning and mental toughness, the X factor of athletic performance.

Use this mountain workout from Morris and you can train there, too—even if you live in Wichita. After your warmup, raise the treadmill grade to 5 to 8 percent (lower for beginners, higher if you're a seasoned vet). Then set the speed to a pace that's about 3 minutes slower than your best mile time. So if you can run a mile in 7 minutes (8.5 mph), you'll set the speed to the equivalent of a 10-minute mile pace, which is 6 mph. Run at that speed and grade for as long as you can maintain conversation in short spurts (three or four words at a time). Once

PEAK
performance

Three ways to master any mountain

No matter how well you've trained indoors, an outdoor course will present new challenges—wind resistance, extreme temperatures, sanitation trucks. There's also a psychological obstacle: University of Virginia scientists found that people tend to judge hills with a 10-degree slant to be about 30 degrees. So hills seem more daunting than the same grade on a treadmill. Learn to tackle them like a pro.

Look ahead. Specifically, 10 feet in front of you. It'll ensure that your upper body and lower body stay aligned. "If you bend forward at the waist, you'll reposition your center of gravity so that you have to fight your own weight as you climb," says Scott Jurek, a seven-time winner of the Western States 100-mile ultraendurance race.

Use baby steps. As you run uphill, count the number of steps you take in 15 seconds. Then multiply that number by 4 to get your stride rate. If it's not above 85, shorten your steps or you'll tire out faster, says Jurek.

Start slow. Trying to go fast up an entire hill may cause you to run out of gas early, says Mindy Solkin, a USA Track and Field Level III certified running coach. The solution: Keep your overall effort level the same, even if you have to slow your pace as you close in on the peak.

you're breathing too hard to talk, shut it down and record your distance. You should strive to run a little farther—even if it's just $\frac{1}{10}$ of a mile—each time you repeat the workout. One to 2 miles is good for starters; make it to 5 and you're ready for the hall of fame.

BY CHRISTOPHER MCDOUGALL

Heed the New Rules of Running

We sent a self-proclaimed "fairly sane runner" to keep pace with the crazies who run 100-mile races. Should he try?

In the land of the ultrafreaks, the man with toenails is a mutant. That's what I discover when I arrive at Grand Targhee Resort, at the foot of Wyoming's Tetons, for the Badwater Ultramarathon Training Camp. For the next 5 days, I'll be working out with a dozen or so adventure racers and extreme endurance athletes as they prepare for the most fearsome footrace on earth: a 135-mile run across Death Valley and up the side of Mount Whitney in the blistering heat of summer.

But, unlike some of the serious badasses here—guys like the Toenail Ripper, the Army Ranger, and Jungle Boy—I'm not interested in running 60 straight hours across a desert in July. Nor do I plan to be hunted by trained killers in a Georgia swamp or race through the Amazon on foot while dodging jaguars and those needle-thin river fish that swim up your penis or have my toenails removed to improve my ultramarathon times.

So, what can I learn from these guys? Well, the secret of lifelong fitness, for starters.

Ultrarunners, after all, are among the most durable, carefully trained athletes on the planet. They're masters of increasing horsepower without blowing the engine. Real endurance, they know, isn't about gutting it out on race day; it's about keeping consistent for years before race day.

Beneath the lunatic appearance of men who are running on roads so hot that their shoes are melting lies a marvel of strategy, nutrition, and innovation. They've had to learn how hard they can punish their bodies without breaking down and how to get the maximum workout in minimum time. They'd never make it to the start unless they knew how to train for months without injury, and they'd never make it to the finish if they weren't experts in muscle care and motivation.

These are lessons that can be applied to any sport, and that's why I'm here: to see if I can break my lifelong cycle of on-again/off-again conditioning and become as body-savvy as a man facing 3 days under a brutal desert sun.

Emulate Girl Power

Day 1 begins with Cameron Diaz, hill repeats, and a puzzle. First, the puzzle: Nearly all the women finish the Leadville Trail 100 Ultramarathon every year, but less than half of the men do. Why?

"Relentless forward motion," says Cameron, who, despite her Hollywood smile and freckly blonde beauty, turns out to be Lisa Smith-Batchen, 45, the legendary ultrarunner who's one of our instructors (www.lisasmithbatchen.com). "Take this hill, for example," she says, as we cruise up a mile-long slope. "I'll bet your instinct is to hammer it, right?"

Well, yeah. And I'm glad she brought that up, because, frankly, I've been a little disappointed. As soon as we start to breathe heavily, we're supposed to walk. Even for a plodder like me, that seems pretty wimpy. But I have to figure Smith-Batchen knows

HARD TRUTH

Percentage of runners who experience some type of injury every year:

50

what she's talking about: She's not only a two-time female Badwater champ and a highly respected endurance coach but also the only American, male or female, ever to win the hideously grueling Marathon des Sables, a 6-day stage race across the Sahara.

By our second ascent, the mastery in Smith-Batchen's hill-climbing method becomes clear. When she walks, she's gliding upward with a rhythm that's as smooth and deceptively technical as a speed skater's: Her pelvis is forward; her shoulders are squared over her belly button; her breathing is a series of metronomic belly puffs; her thumbs are pistoning straight back and forth to her hips.

When I throttle back and mimic her technique, I'm surprised to find I move about as fast as I would if I were running but with a fraction of the effort. At the top, I can shift right back to a run without having to drop my hands to my knees to suck wind.

"The mistake lots of guys make is hammering themselves, or each other, and then crashing," Smith-Batchen explains. They think it makes them look tough, but it can actually be a sign of self-doubt: If you're

confident that you've prepared well, you don't need to prove it on every hill. Men who do may be unconsciously prepping themselves with an excuse for not finishing. Fly-and-die guys eventually end up missing workouts, thanks to tendinitis and hamstring pulls, or find ways to back off before things get tough.

That's one reason ultra women have such a great finishing percentage, Smith-Batchen says. Their true challenger is in the mirror, they realize, so they tend to run on brains. As she is making this point, I recall with a cringe how many times I've flamed out of hoops games, trail runs, and weight circuits, usually because I started writing checks with my cojones that my muscles couldn't cash.

Think with Your D---

"Before I start a race, I think, *Okay, where's my penis?*"

Ray Zahab is not nearly the horndog this question makes him out to be. At 33, he's already won an individual title in the Arctic Yukon Ultra; a team title in the 120-mile Jungle Marathon; and third place in the

Can acupressure work as well as acupuncture for joint pain?

Yes, it's worth a try, says *Men's Health* alternative-medicine advisor Keith DeOrio, MD. Both utilize meridians—invisible energy pathways that connect various points in the body to the internal organs. Acupressure can allow the body's energy pathways to flow more smoothly, which may result in a reduction of joint pain.

Trans 333, a nonstop, 200-mile footrace across the Ténéré Desert in Niger.

Today, he's leading an afternoon session on core conditioning, demonstrating how a few posture tweaks can have an amazing effect on short-burst speed and long-range resilience. By keeping your body weight properly balanced, Zahab says, you can increase gravitational pull to accelerate, and decrease it to diminish the strain on your joints and tendons.

The key is your core—the lower-back and transverse abdominal muscles that girdle your midsection. Most people have developed the bad habit of striding out long when they want to go fast and putting their heads down to grind it out when they're tired. It may feel natural, but they're actually working against themselves by slopping their body mass all over the place. When you hunch over, you're directing your weight downward instead of forward. When you lunge out with a long stride and land on your heels, you're really throwing your weight back behind you.

Instead, imagine you're pedaling a unicycle: Keep your shoulders plumb-lined over your hips and kick back with your feet instead of reaching out. To speed up, lean forward from the ankles instead of bending forward from the waist; you'll create a light, controlled fall instead of a muscle-intensive series of pushoffs.

"You should use this anytime, in any activity," Zahab says: hiking, biking, sprinting down the basketball court. Besides going faster with less effort, you'll preserve your

legs by stacking your weight over your strong, protectively arched midfeet, instead of crashing down on the sensitive nerves in your heels or the fragile tendons in your toes.

Zahab has two methods to make sure he's properly positioned. First is the toe tilt, which he does just before starting to run: If he can lift his toes without rocking back, he's balanced. The second is the penis test—a handy, in-motion diagnostic that determines whether his hips are jutting forward enough. Whenever he feels that his biomechanics are getting sloppy, Zahab glances down at his appendage to make sure his pelvis isn't lagging. "If it's up front," he says, "you're fine." As I follow his advice, I notice a strange sensation in my calves and ankles: no sensation. For the first time in weeks, my Achilles aren't aching. Not too brightly, I ran a lot of miles and biked a lot of hills to prepare for camp, which meant I arrived here with overworked, twinging calves. The relief

I feel when I fully straighten my spinal column is so dramatic, I soon use Zahab's penis test to coin a mental reminder: "Limp, owww! Erect, ahhh."

Meanwhile, I'm surprised to see two other guys practicing just as intently. One is Jim Simone, the former Army Ranger turned ultrarunner. As part of his combat training, Simone spent 3 days crossing a swamp while evading a squad of Special Forces soldiers. Since then, he's run marathons all over the world and survived desert ultras on two continents. Next to him is Marshall Ulrich, also known as the Toenail Ripper (to me, at least). In the documentary about Badwater, *Running on the Sun*, Ulrich is the guy who appears on camera explaining why he decided his toenails were dead weight and had them surgically removed.

Watching these two badasses taking Zahab's advice so obediently is all the con-

vincing I need; if their techniques need correction, mine has a long way to go.

Create Your Own Hell

On day 3, we studied the case of Frank McKinney. McKinney was a 41-year-old real-estate magnate who'd never run a marathon and lived in the eternal springtime of Delray Beach, Florida, a good 100 miles from a decent hill. And in 6 months, he would have to run five back-to-back marathons across Death Valley, culminating in a nearly 9,000-foot climb up Mount Whitney.

So how could he learn to run mountains without any mountains? Easy. If he couldn't put the resistance in front of him, he'd put it behind him. He tied a rope around an SUV tire, clipped the rope to a weight belt, and dragged it back and forth across an inter-coastal bridge. He also created his own Death Valley simulator: He stuck a treadmill in a spare bedroom and surrounded it with heat lamps, a space heater, a dehumidifier, and massive fans to reproduce baking winds (though the fans sort of got ruined when his wife tried to create a desert storm by sprinkling them with sand).

The plan worked. In 6 months, McKinney transformed himself from a weekend tennis player into a member of the elite club of Badwater finishers. "It's amazing how much you can adapt to your environment if you focus on the essentials of what your body really needs to learn," says Smith-Batchen. Take mountain biking and trail running, she says: Besides raw conditioning, the crucial technical skills you need are quick hands

Notes from Mile 263

Last fall, Dean Karnazes, *Men's Health*'s "Behind the Burn" columnist, ran 350 miles without stopping in 80 hours and 44 minutes. We can't recommend that. But we can all learn from his tips on going the distance.

Run stairs to build strength. Too many runners don't think about strength—in their legs and lungs—when facing an endurance test. Find a staircase or stadium, ideally with more than 100 steps, for a weekly workout. Start by running to the top a single step at a time and walking back down. Five sets will leave you sore. Work your way up to 10 sets. Next phase: two steps at a time, walking down, five sets. Final phase: two steps up, single steps down, running both ways, working up from five to 10 sets. Keep at it till you can repeat this routine 3 or 4 days a week.

Run quicker, not harder. A higher cadence, or turnover rate (how quickly you put one foot in front of the other), can make you faster with less effort. Elite distance runners stay in the range of 185 to 200 steps per minute. Varying your cadence can conserve energy and shift the load among different muscles. As you fatigue and slow down, focus on cadence, not speed. This might mean taking shorter,

quicker steps. Experiment in training. A rule of thumb: If your stride rate falls below 150 to 160 steps per minute, shorten your stride and increase turnover.

Work to recover. Big distance can mean big hurt. The day after a long run, you must force yourself to exercise. You don't have to run—try a bike ride, a swim, or just a nice walk. The movement increases bloodflow, clearing the by-products of intense exercise from your muscles and helping restore flexibility. Carry bottled water and drink all day. Your hydrated cells will thank you.

and feet. Jumping rope works for that.

Smith-Batchen takes us outside for a brisk, muscle-trembling series of calisthenics. As a working mother, Smith-Batchen is an expert at filling the unforgiving lunch hour with 60 minutes of running, jumping rope, and plyometric hopping. She borrows her routines from a sport that's nearly as ancient as running: boxing. It makes sense; boxing demands consummate conditioning

and leaves no margin for error.

"Who needs dumbbells when you have a park bench?" she shouts as she leads us through a series of incline-pushup salutes. (Pushing up against the bench with two arms, we then twist at the hip and raise one arm until it's pointing at the sky.) For the tired malcontents among us, Smith-Batchen is ready with a shouted explanation: "You'll need that triceps power to piston your arms

If I'm on my feet for a long time, I get leg cramps at night. What can I do to stop this?

This is exactly what happens to soldiers and Buckingham Palace guards. The problem is poor circulation. Wear soft-soled shoes with cushion inserts if you're going to be standing for long periods. Every 30 to 60 minutes, do toe raises: three sets of 20. When you get home, massage and stretch your legs. A nice hot bath can help, too.

when you're making your third 3,000-foot ascent in 6 hours. And if your pecs aren't strong, your chest is going to cave around your lungs when you get tired." Calisthenics, she points out, makes you body-aware; you have to pay careful attention to form and balance, rather than heaving iron around.

I'm quickly feeling a change come over me. It's only day 3, and already I'm feeling differently about my toenails.

Four months later, I barely recognize myself from the waist down. I'm running longer and harder than I ever have in my life, but the impact is virtually nonexistent. I used to think a marathon was a big deal; now I run one just about every month and still have enough energy to get behind the mower for a few hours or goof around with the kids.

Strangest of all, this surge in my workload hasn't caused a single injury, and it's cleared up the ones I already had. All those nagging foot and Achilles problems that bugged me for years? Gone. Whenever I feel the slightest twinge in my calves or hamstrings, I think of Ray Zahab, check my package position, and adjust. That always takes care of it. Of course, I haven't completely gone over to the ultrafreak side; there's no way you're going to catch me running across Death Valley in July. But there is a 50-miler in Mexico that's looking kind of tempting . . .

BY ROBERT DOS REMEDIOS, CSCS

Reinvent Your Wheels

Pay attention to your legs
to build a ripped new body
from the ground up

Training Tips

I'm a runner looking to stay motivated. Is there a masters circuit for track?

Yes, for competitive athletes 35 and older. Age brackets are 35 to 39, 40 to 44, 45 to 49, 50 to 54, and so on. Local, regional, and national competitions are available. To get involved, visit www.masterstrack.com and the training forums at www.bestlifeonline.com.

I'm 4 months into training for a marathon, and I swear my "guys" are closer to my body than they used to be. Can running make a man's testicles rise?

This is one of those "testicle myths" that have no basis in real medicine. It's impressive that you've noticed some shifting of your testicles, but the truth is that the scrotal sac can change hang depths depending on several factors, including temperature, time of day, and activity, but not fitness level. Don't be alarmed. Your guys might just want some attention.

I like to run 3 miles right after I lift, but does doing this stop my muscles from growing?

Yes. If your primary goal is to pack on muscle, the only thing that should follow your workout is a protein shake. But if you exercise purely for fitness, then running afterward is a good thing. For the best blend of fitness and strength workouts, try interval training. Run as hard as you can for 30 to 60 seconds, followed by 2 to 3 minutes of very easy jogging or fast walking, then repeat for 3 miles.

I'm training for a marathon and don't want to lose muscle. How can I preserve it?

Don't sweat it. You could do a couple of total-body workouts a week on off days, but lean mass means more work for your body when you run. That's why great marathoners have slight frames. Focus on nutrition and warm up with exercises for hip and trunk stability, like lunges and crunches. When you've completed your marathon, hit the weights hard, and your mass will jump right back.

I run about 60 miles a week, but my legs look like twigs. How can I beef them up?

Here's a plan that will pack lean muscle onto those chicken legs in just 6 weeks. Ever notice the wheels on world-class sprinters? Sprinting builds

muscle, so replace two long runs every week with intense speed intervals of 100 to 400 yards. Run a total of 600 to 800 yards for each workout (for example, eight 100-yard sprints or two 400-yard sprints). Run at close to maximum intensity for each sprint. Also, do lower-body exercises twice a week, which is enough to help you add muscle but not so much that you won't be able to completely recover between workouts. Do squats and lunges using a challenging weight; do three to five sets, with five to eight repetitions per set. This time-tested, effective combination will get you the results you're after.

How do I prep for a high-altitude event when I live in the plains?

The most practical solution is to travel to the event as far in advance as possible to allow your body to acclimate. Other-wise, you're prone to "sidewalk syndrome." That is, one minute you're fine, exerting yourself the same way you would in the lowlands, and the next you're lying on the sidewalk from lack of oxygen. Though it can take several weeks to adjust fully,

changes will begin within a couple of days.

What causes weakness and dizziness while you're running?

One possibility is exercise-induced high blood pressure, says cardiologist John Elefteria-des, MD. You may seem fit, but your arteries can't handle the strain of exercise, so your blood pressure rises. This can be genetic, and it usually doesn't have any other symptoms. Many in the medical community think high blood pressure during exercise is itself a risk factor for heart disease and may predate the onset of typical hypertension. See a cardiologist about your symptoms.

Why use a heart-rate monitor during my workout?

To keep you honest and to honestly track your progress. "People can fool themselves about how hard they're working, but a heart-rate monitor doesn't lie," says Alan Stein, CSCS, co-owner of Elite Athlete Training Systems, in Rockville, Maryland. Without one, it's impossible to tell if you've reached the 65 to 90 percent of your maximum heart rate needed for a successful

cardio workout. (Find your max heart rate by subtracting your age from 220.)

A heart-rate monitor can also be a tool for personalized interval training—an ideal way to burn calories and build endurance. "Using a heart-rate monitor, you can push yourself to hit 85 or 90 percent of your max heart rate, keep it there for 20 to 30 seconds, then come back down to 60 percent before you attempt the next rep," says Stein. This ensures a more personalized workout, as opposed to following a generic interval routine—hard for 30 seconds, moderate for a minute, and so on. Pick up a monitor with a few basic func-tions, like Polar's F11 model ($160; www.polarusa.com), which shows your heart rate, average heart rate after an exercise session, and calories burned. It also sounds an alarm when you drop below your target heart rate.

PART SIX

On any given day, 20 percent of men participate in sports. We hope you're one of them. Sports offer the best of both worlds—a great workout and a great deal of fun. What's your pleasure? In this chapter, we focus on the big three: cycling, golf, and swimming. But you can apply the exercises and strategies you learn here to any sport—or even the game of life.

First, we aim to keep you in the game by offering 85 tips to keep your body game-ready. Then you'll learn six simple steps to improve your cycling from a cyclist who studied with the pros at Georgia's Brasstown Bald. Next, you'll discover six tricks to shrink your golf handicap from PGA pro Todd Hamilton. Then learn how to leave everyone in your wake with our seven-step swimming plan—and get into phenomenal shape in the process: It really is easy to paddle your way to an eight-pack. Later, in our at-home dumbbell workout, you'll raise your game with three simple moves.

These tips and tricks should help you have your best year ever on the course, in the pool, or wherever it is that you play.

REPORTING BY MATT BEAN, KATE DAILEY, SCOTT QUILL, PHILLIP RHODES, AND DAVID SCHIPPER

Stay in the Game

85 tips to keep your body ready for every game

They shoot lame horses. Lame athletes, they send to physical therapy. That's why we're fans of not getting hurt in the first place. Here are dozens of ways to reach the finish line and, best of all, the bar—to brag about it. You don't want to waste your best stories on an ER nurse, after all.

1. Stop and start to fight muscle strains. Sprint-based sports such as baseball and basketball churn out a lot of lower-body muscle strains. The fix: stop-and-start drills. "If you train your body to do something that's specific to your sport, then that training should take you through a full season," says Arizona Diamondbacks veteran shortstop Royce Clayton. Try his drill: Run 40 yards at about 70 percent of your maximum effort, slow to a jog for 10 yards, then pick it up again for another 40 yards. Repeat four or five times. You'll be conditioned to sprint to first base, slow down, and charge for second, or run out for a pass if your teammate steals the basketball. There's glory for the first man downcourt.

2. Crouch, tiger. Seventy percent of ACL injuries occur when players pivot or land awkwardly after a jump. Hitting the ground with your knees bent instead of nearly straight greatly reduces the risk, according to a report published in the *Journal of the American Academy of Orthopaedic Surgeons*.

3. Figure the heatstroke equation. Heatstroke harms many an unwary athlete. Do the math: If the temperature and relative humidity combined equal 160, stay cool and hydrated, says Dave Janda, MD, director of

the Institute for Preventative Sports Medicine. If the number tops 180, exercise indoors or move to Canada.

4. Protect your nose. Once you wipe out, your surfboard becomes a weapon; boards inflict 55 percent of all surfing injuries. Make it less dangerous by applying a rubber "nose guard" to your board ($20; www. ronjons.com). Acting as a front bumper, it wraps around and caps the pointy front end of your board. "If it hits you, it doesn't really hurt," says pro windsurfer Tristan Boxford.

5. Replace your funky equipment. Stressing joints that are out of alignment, also referred to as overuse, is a major cause of sports injuries. Even a bike or racket that's

not properly sized for you can cause improper movement patterns that spawn overuse injuries, says Mark Verstegen, MS, CSCS, director of performance for the NFL Players Association. The extra hundred bucks you spend at the pro shop can save you 10 times that at the orthopedic doctor's office. The choice is yours, sport.

6. Correct your funky swing. "If your technique isn't right, you'll predispose your body to injury," says Edward Laskowski, MD, codirector of the Mayo Clinic Sports Medicine Center. That's why you need to seek advice from the golf pro, the basketball coach, the trainer, the mountain guide. MJ and Shaq didn't win NBA titles until they met Phil Jackson, after all; you're only as good as the advice you get.

7. Just add water. "Seventy-five percent of muscle mass is made up of fluid," says Jackie Berning, RD, nutritional consultant for the Cleveland Indians and Denver Broncos. If you don't drink enough, your risk of strains, sprains, and pulled muscles escalates.

8. Change your oil. Omega-3 fatty acids fight inflammation just like aspirin. (But the sources—walnuts, salmon—taste better.) That means less pain, more gains.

9. Go on green. Leafy green vegetables and citrus fruits boost the blood's alkaline levels, which helps heal wounds faster, says Gay Riley, MS, RD, CCN, author of *The Pocket Personal Trainer.* They'll also make your blood less acidic, which cuts inflammation.

10. Give yourself a C. "Collagen is abundant in connective tissues, tendons, bones, and muscles," says Riley. Vitamin C is a key component of your body's collagen recipe.

11. Give yourself another C: calcium. A study from Brigham and Women's Hospital found that injured athletes typically consumed 25 to 40 percent less calcium than their uninjured counterparts—i.e., the winners.

12. Do it your whey. Glutathione, an antioxidant, protects your body in many ways, says Riley, and whey powder helps you make more of it. Whey is also the most readily absorbed source of branched-chain amino acids—microscopic muscle-repair kits.

13. Chug a Coke (or antioxidant-packed iced tea). In a University of Georgia study, cyclists who downed 10 milligrams of caffeine per kilogram of body weight before a 30-minute ride had significantly less thigh pain than those who took a placebo.

14. Make your warmup multidirectional. Think about the wild gyrations you perform during one turnover from offense to defense in basketball. If your groin, back, and leg muscles aren't ready, you'll pull up in pain. Before the game, run backward, forward, sideways, and in quick combos of all directions.

15. Videotape your mistakes, just like Pam and Paris. The camera knows and sees all, Dr. Laskowski says: "But only when you have a knowledgeable person to interpret it." Which is where that coach or pro comes in.

16. Swing a racket with your legs. "People forget to use their legs when they're hitting their serve or other strokes," says Doug Spreen, ATC, trainer of tennis pro Andy

PEAK performance

Walk This Way

It's great that you jog around the gym to warm up for hoops, but an "active warmup" works better. "It helps improve your dynamic flexibility, as well as prepare your muscles, tendons, ligaments, and joints for the game," says Alan Stein, CSCS, a basketball strength-and-conditioning coach and co-owner of Elite Athlete Training Systems. Perform each movement for half the length of the basketball court, switching at the half-court line.

Over the fence. Raise your left knee as high as you can and swing it behind you, rotating to the left as if you were stepping backward over a fence. Repeat with your right leg and slowly walk backward.

Lunge walk. Step forward into a lunge position with your left leg, lowering your right knee almost to the ground (ankles, knees, hips, and shoulders square and torso upright). Rotate your upper body to your left and hold, then repeat to your right. Face forward and rise. Lunge with your right leg and repeat the move.

Walking kicks. Raise your left thigh till it's parallel to the ground, then kick your left heel up and back toward your butt before stepping forward with your left leg. Repeat with your right leg and move your feet as quickly as possible.

Pointer. Take a step with your left leg, keeping your knees locked and your toes pointing upward. Reach down with your right hand and touch your toes. Rise and repeat with your right leg, touching your toes with your left hand.

Knee hug. Raise your left knee, grab it with both hands, and hug it to your chest. Release and repeat with your right leg. Start slowly, but go faster as it becomes comfortable.

Frankenstein march. Stretch your arms out straight in front of you, fingers extended. Raise your left knee as you begin your step, straightening your leg out as if to touch your toes with your left hand (bonus points if you can). Bring it down and repeat with your right leg, trying to touch your toes with your right hand.

Roddick. For instance, when you toss the ball up for a serve, you'll stress your lower back if you're not using your legs. Bend your knees and push up and through the serve with your legs, Spreen says. You'll gather power from the strongest part of your body.

17. Loosen your shoulders. An injured rotator cuff can shut down a shoulder, says Spreen, who suggests adding external and internal rotation stretching to protect your cuffs. External: Stand with your right arm straight out to the side and parallel to the floor. Bend your elbow so your arm forms a right angle and your forearm points straight up. Keeping your elbow in place, move your hand back until you feel slight tension in

your shoulder. Internal: Same as above, except your forearm should point straight down toward the floor at the start. Hold each stretch for 30 seconds.

18. Hit the pool early. Inhaling organic material, such as hair, skin, and urine, can cause breathing problems. Schedule your lap sessions early: Fewer people in the pool means less splashing and less of their debris left behind in the water.

19. Arm yourself to the teeth. Men who wear custom-fitted mouth guards reduce their risk of dental injuries by 82 percent, according to a study from the University of North Carolina at Chapel Hill. Lay out the money for a custom-fitted guard and it'll last for years. So will your smile.

20. Smooth out tendon problems. Ask your doctor about ultrasound needle therapy. The minimally invasive procedure uses ultrasound to guide a needle, which doctors use to smooth bone, break up calcifications, and fix scar tissue. Sixty-five percent of patients who underwent the therapy saw improvement, and a session takes only 5 to 15 minutes.

21. Buy running shoes after work. Shop at night, when your feet are swollen after a day of pounding, advises Chad Asplund, MD, a physician at Eisenhower Army Medical Center in Georgia and a running-shoe researcher. It approximates how big your feet will be after the first 3 miles of your run.

22. Exercise off road. Unstable surfaces train stable ankles.

23. Beat the heat. Humid environments—i.e., anywhere south of, say, Maine and east

PEAK
performance

Put a Positive Spin on It
You may never launch a football as far as Favre, but you can toss a spiral as tight as the shorts on an Eagles cheerleader. It all starts with your grip, says former Vikings QB and current ESPN analyst Sean Salisbury.

Grab the end of the ball and position your ring finger and pinky over the laces (up to the first knuckle of each). "This is where the natural spiral spin will come from," says Salisbury. Next, with your elbow at a 90-degree angle, hold the ball a few inches above and to the side of your shoulder. Now, in one smooth motion, draw your hand back behind your shoulder and then bring it forward, releasing the ball with a snap of your wrist as soon as it passes your head. The back of your hand should face your target as you follow through.

Still wafting wounded ducks? Read the writing on the ball: If it says "NCAA" or "College," spike it; this type is fatter and harder to throw than an NFL ball ($80; www.wilson.com).

of Colorado—only make asthma worse, as former Pittsburgh Steelers running back Jerome Bettis well knows. He passed out on the field in 1997 from an asthma attack. "You couldn't just react to the problem. You have to make sure it's controlled," he says. He couldn't change midday practice times, but you can. Run early. Temperatures are lower, and so are the humidity and ozone levels that can induce an attack. (Find more tips online at www.lungusa.org.)

24. Control inflammation with bromelain (120 milligrams per day). "It's almost like putting a chemical cold pack on a bruise or sprain," says Chris Foley, MD, a professor at the University of Minnesota College of Pharmacy. Extremely safe and inexpensive, bromelain has been shown to reduce swelling, bruising, healing time, and pain following injuries. A 2002 British study found that it relieved mild knee pain, as well.

25. Shore up weak tissue with glucosamine sulfate (daily amount: 1,500 milligrams). Think of it as adding cement to a creaky foundation, says David Grotto, RD, director of nutrition at the Block Center for Integrative Cancer Care. Glucosamine creates polymers called glucosaminal glycans (GAG) that build and strengthen the tissues, preventing tears. Try pairing it with chondroitin, which promotes GAG formation and inhibits degradation enzymes in connective tissue.

26. Limit oxidation with green-tea extract (up to 800 milligrams per day). When athletes train and compete, there's a whole lot of cellular combustion taking

place. "That combustion has by-products, and if you're not taking care of those by-products, they can be harmful over time," says Dr. Foley, who warns that this could even lead to a higher tendency toward cancer. Antioxidants from green tea can manage your body's oxidative stress.

27. Encourage recovery with SAM-e (work up to 1,200 milligrams per day). Methylation—a chemical process that helps your body build connective tissue—is important in muscle recovery, inflammation control, and muscle support and stability, says Dr. Foley. If you take NSAIDs (nonsteroidal anti-inflammatory drugs, such as aspirin and ibuprofen), all they do is block

they are, and the better your body's going to react to a hit," Bettis says.

29. Assess the course. It doesn't matter whether you're biking, paddling, or skiing—take a dry run down any route first. "You see a lot of paddlers injured because they just don't know what they're getting into," says Tao Berman, a world-class kayaker who holds the record for running the highest waterfall (98.4 feet) in a kayak. "If I look at a fall and think I'm not going to be able to control the way I land, then I walk away." As should you.

30. Take the path of least resistance. Crash landings require stuntmanlike instincts, whether you're smacking the water or the turf. "You want to be as aerodynamic as possible when you hit," says Berman. "Just before impact, I lean forward against the front of my kayak so I don't take a huge hit to my chest as I reenter the water." Use the same technique on a bike or in touch football. "I don't stop short; I just go with the fall and let my body roll through the impact," he says.

31. Practice hard. Performance anxiety narrows your peripheral vision by as much as 3 degrees and slows reaction time by 119 milliseconds, according to the *Journal of Sports Sciences*. When the going gets tough, the tough rely on the skills they've practiced. It helps keep them cool under pressure, widening their range of vision so they see that linebacker coming and react within milliseconds.

32. Socialize after exercise. Lack of social support upped risk of injury in a University of Washington study.

postworkout inflammation. Pop SAM-e instead; it fuels methylation to provide benefits beyond the effect of NSAIDs.

28. Face your attacker. In a lot of sports, it's not whether you'll be nailed—it's whether you'll be able to absorb the blow. Bettis did a footwork drill based on a Latin dance move called the carioca to maintain his agility and face linemen squarely. Try it: Move laterally along a straight line, using crossover steps. Facing forward with your shoulders squared and both hands held out in front as if to absorb a tackle, swivel your hips from side to side, rotating to face the sideline. "The more relaxed your hips are, the more responsive

33. Use a light grip. Gripping a golf club should feel like holding a bird. "Most wrist and elbow injuries occur because people are not gripping the club lightly enough," says Randy Myers, director of fitness at Sea Island Golf Club in Georgia. To get the feel, swing two clubs at once; it can't be done with a tight grip.

34. Go ahead, sprinkle salt. Especially the night before your August century ride. Extra sodium helps you retain water and stay hydrated while exercising in high temperatures. But stay away from salt pills; they may do more harm to your blood pressure than good for your race.

35. Try this before a triathlon. To avoid training strains, two-time world champion Ironman Tim DeBoom builds endurance by concentrating on the bike—a low-impact way to push yourself. When the race starts in a mad, watery scramble, he gives the competition some distance: "Just pull out to the side and be a little less aggressive." That way, you won't have to learn by broken bones in the face—as DeBoom did.

36. Cancel the victory cigars. A study of army recruits found that smokers were nearly 50 percent more likely than clean-lunged privates to suffer fractures, sprains, and other injuries. Smoking may interfere with wound healing and muscle repair.

37. Slide safely into third. Aim up and over the side of the bag, advises Robert Frederick, MD, team physician for the Philadelphia Phillies. "Slide over it so your foot or hand is not catching on it." If your slide comes to a sudden stop, your joints take most of the impact.

38. And avoid the guy sliding into second. "Usually, when you see a guy get flipped, it's because he went outside the bag to make the throw," says shortstop Royce Clayton. "If you can't jump and throw, use the bag to protect you." Stand directly behind the bag: "You may not be able to throw [to turn a double play], but at least he's not going to get a piece of you."

39. Check the ozone levels. When you hear the phrase "ozone alert day," move your workout indoors. A study in the *Lancet* found that people who exercise in high ozone conditions are three times more likely to develop asthma than those who skip workouts on those days.

40. Don't run in wet shoes. Soggy midsoles have 40 to 50 percent less shock-absorbing capability than dry sneaks, Dr. Asplund says. But don't toss your shoes in the dryer; heat can degrade cushioning and support components.

41. Know how to fall. Learning to snowboard is a snap—for your wrists. When you fall, let your butt and back share the

HARD TRUTH
Number of men who play touch football:
1 in 2

impact with your forearms. And wear wrist guards; they may not look sexy, but neither will a cast and sling. The coolest we've seen: K2's new EXO 6.0 ($10; www.k2skates.com).

42. Buy a softer hardball. The RIF5SL baseball ($5) reduces injury risk by 23 percent. Little League Baseball's governing body has approved its use, and it's optional at all age levels. When researchers at Tufts University removed the ball's labeling, few players could tell the difference between the softer ball and standard ones.

43. Unwind the ankle tape. It loosens after 10 minutes of play, according to the *American Journal of Sports Medicine.* Researchers found that people who wore ankle braces returned to full participation after an injury 2 days sooner than those who were taped.

44. Brace that sprain. And keep it braced for at least 6 months, advises the National Center for Injury Prevention and Control. Most foot and ankle injuries are caused by incomplete healing of prior hurts. Chuck Kimmel, president of the National Athletic Trainers' Association, recommends a lightweight lace-up brace (try McDavid's, $25, www.mcdavidusa.com).

45. A brace isn't a cure. Warning: A University of Iowa study found that athletes who wear ankle braces are 61 percent more likely to be injured. Lesson: If you brace a bum wheel, it's still bum. Before you play hard, heal first.

46. Balance your muscles. Your dominant side tends to be stronger, leading to muscular imbalances, which can result in injuries, Dr. Laskowski says. Lift with dumbbells, which isolate each side and balance weaknesses.

47. Avoid cart-required golf courses. Walking the course will keep your back and hips loose between shots, helping to prevent muscle pulls and strains, Myers says.

48. Stretch your swing muscles. If you refuse to give up the golf cart, Myers suggests using it as a stretching tool: Stand facing the side of the cart, about a foot away. With your knees slightly bent, reach out and grab the handle on the side. Keeping your arms fully extended, sit back so your buttocks and hips extend out away from the cart. You should feel a stretch in the lower part of your back. Hold for 10 seconds. Repeat twice every hole.

49. Give unsexy muscles their due. Men work their chests and biceps and forget that the shoulder is a balanced joint that needs strong muscles on both sides, says Dr. Frederick. That makes your shoulders more susceptible to muscle strains when you pitch a fastball or slam a serve. For every set of chest presses you do, perform a set of seated rows.

50. Run for your life! Thirty-six percent of lightning deaths occur during recreational activities.

51. Buy one pair at a time. According to Dr. Asplund, running shoes lose cushioning—even if they've never been worn—after 1 to 2 years. Once you start wearing them on the road, they'll lose 50 percent of their shock absorption by 250 miles.

52. Play tennis on clay or grass. "Natural surfaces are kinder to your body," says Kathleen Stroia, ATC, vice president of sports sciences and medicine for the Sony Ericsson Women's Tennis Association Tour. Plus, soft surfaces absorb less heat, reducing heat-stroke risk.

53. Beware eyeball busters. Basketball is responsible for the most eye injuries, according to the University of Michigan Kellogg Eye Center. Our favorite orb protectors: Rec-Specs Maxx line ($100, www.libertyoptical. net), which meet international safety standards without looking too, you know, goggly.

54. Stop the music. Unplug your iPod before starting down the slopes. "[Music] slows you down mentally," says skier Bode Miller, the 2005 World Cup champion. "You need to process what's ahead of you so you have time to avoid danger." Mountain

bikers and trail runners should unplug as well.

55. Work out in water. Swimming is the perfect low-impact alternative to running. But what if you can't stand swimming? Dr. Laskowski recommends weighted-vest running in the pool. It's low impact for your legs but provides an amazing heart workout. "Even walking around chest deep is great exercise," he says.

56. Obey the 15-minute rule after a hit to the head. If you've seen stars for that long, you're out of it—the game, that is, says Edward Wojtys, MD, a professor of surgery at the University of Michigan. You'll need 10 to 14 days to recover. Avoid any activity that's likely to jar your head. (So unload those Ozzfest tickets.)

57. Strap your boys in. A recent study in the *Clinical Journal of Sport Medicine* found that 47 percent of high school and college male athletes involved in contact sports do not wear any kind of genital protection. The upshot? These Darwin Award winners are less likely to breed and pass on their genes.

58. Antifreeze your lungs. Inhaling freezing air can inflame airways, which may

lead to asthma attacks, according to Finnish researchers. In icy weather, consider donning a Polar Wrap ($30, www.polarwrap.com). A built-in device uses your body heat to warm the air you breathe before it enters your body.

59. Become a multisport warrior. Love your weekly tennis match? It may not love you back. Excessive repetition of motion increases your risk of developing arthritis. The simplest solution: Change your signature serve. Modifying your movement can help you avoid repeated microtears or fractures.

60. Simulate, but don't emulate. Nobody's asking you to quit your favorite sport. But if you want to last at it, bring

similar sports into the mix. "You want to cross-train those muscles in a different way so they adapt in a different way," Dr. Laskowski says. Natural pairings: skiing and soccer, swimming and martial arts, running and cycling, tennis and hoops.

61. Train your brain to heal your ankle. Training sensory receptors in your ankles can help prevent recurrent injury, according to research from the Netherlands. Using a wobble board strengthens what the researchers call proprioception: the subconscious bond between your nerves and the muscles that do your brain's bidding. Try standing on the board for 5 minutes a day—say, while you're reading the sports section. When that becomes easy, balance with your eyes closed. (And listen to sports on your XM handheld.)

62. Train your brain to stay upright. Here's another good reason to invest in a wobble board. "It helps you work on maintaining your sense of balance and keeping your center of gravity low for surfing," says Boxford. "It also requires you to move your ankles in a similar fashion to what you'll be doing on the water." Simply standing on the

Wish Granted

Early in his career, fans knew Grant Hill for his arm: He threw the three-quarters-court Hail Mary pass to Christian Laettner, whose shot then lifted Duke over Kentucky in the 1992 NCAA tournament. But for the past 5 years, fans have known Hill for his ankle. His left one. The one that's had five surgeries—and forced the Orlando Magic forward to miss 281 of a possible 328 regular-season games in the 4 years before the 2004–'05 season.

That painful progression brought him back to the scene of his college triumphs—Durham, North Carolina—to the offices of orthopedic surgeon James Nunley, MD. "After three surgeries, people had written me off," Hill says.

Dr. Nunley says the key was identifying an aggravating bone spur and a genetic bow Hill had through his leg and ankle, making it harder for the ankle to heal. "The normal ankle tends to go out slightly. His turned in. If the front end of a car isn't aligned, the tire won't wear properly; his ankle wasn't lined up properly," Dr. Nunley says. "I proposed to him that we go in and break his heel to realign his foot," he says.

The surgery was successful—and Hill, after spending the 2003–'04 season rehabilitating, came back with a career year in 2004–'05. Even though a kick in the shin sidelined Hill at the end of the season, Dr. Nunley wasn't terribly concerned.

"I wanted to come back and play at a high level," says Hill. "I'm not conservative in how I play. I'm falling, I'm jumping into cameramen, I'm playing fearless out there." And perhaps that's the biggest testimony of all to this man who lost half a decade to his injuries. His gut-check play in the 2004–05 season was also peerless: He averaged nearly 20 points a game and was named an all-star.

"It's about making it back well," he says.

Comeback Strategies

Strengthen the ankle. Use this exercise: Lie on your side on a bench and let your feet hang over the edge. Bend your bottom leg so it's behind you. Flex your top foot toward you in a curling motion (like a wrist curl, but with your ankle), then release. To gain more strength, tie your shoelaces together and hang the shoes over your foot before you curl.

Go in stages. The goal of rehab is to regain motion, then build strength, then move on to sport-specific training. Plan and chart your progress. "That's what we did with Grant," Dr. Nunley says. "First we had to heal the bone. Then we had to restore motion in the ankle and toe joints. Then we had to build the muscle strength."

Shock Absorbers

This sports gear takes a beating so you don't have to

Sprint uphill. This treadmill tilts to a full 50 percent incline, boosting your workout while cutting knee-jarring impact. (NordicTrack Incline Trainer X10, $2,300, www.nordictrack.com)

Run naturally. Conventional running shoes make your foot muscles lazy. The segmented soles on these training aids are designed to mimic the experience of barefoot running—without all the tetanus—which helps you build a stronger stride. (Nike Free running shoes, $85, www.nike.com)

Drive better. Thermoplastic inserts in these Callaway irons absorb vibration from the titanium clubface. The bonus: a crisp feel and more control. (Callaway Big Bertha Fusion irons, $1,280, www.callawaygolf.com)

Lighten the load. Flex zones built into this racket add control by preventing the vibration that causes stiffer rackets to jar out of alignment with your hand. It'll keep your elbow happy, too. (Head Flexpoint racket, $200, www.head.com)

Ride longer. Mountain-bike technology smoothes the ride in this road warrior. Potholes be damned. (Cannondale Synapse road bike, $3,200 to $4,400, www.cannondale.com)

board is great practice for sports in which balance is key: skiing, trail running, surfing, golf.

63. Wash your strawberries. Superpowered infections like MRSA (methicillin-resistant *Staphylococcus aureus*) are tough to treat with antibiotics, but the wounds they enter through aren't. Clean all cuts thoroughly with soap and water, apply an antibiotic ointment such as Neosporin, and then keep them covered and dry.

64. Don't overextend yourself on blocks and dunks. "Keep a 15-degree bend in your elbow when going for a block or a dunk," says Tim Grover, owner of Attack Athletics in Chicago and trainer to many NBA players, such as Michael Jordan and Antoine Walker. Overextending your arm makes you prone to injuries.

65. Protect your metatarsals. Add arch supports to your basketball shoes. It'll cut down on pressure on the outer edge of your foot—stress fracture central. Over-the-counter insoles earn a good grade from the American Orthopaedic Foot and Ankle Society, and they'll save you a hundred bucks, compared with custom inserts. Try Montrail's Enduro Stabilizing insoles ($20; www.montrail.com).

66. Eliminate the heel strikes. When you land after a jump, make sure it's toes first, then heel. "If you land either flat-footed or on your heels, you'll be putting a lot of stress on your Achilles tendons and may cause your knees to hyperextend," Grover says.

67. Keep a cool head for a sound body. Researchers found that athletes with high levels of stress off the field are five times more likely to experience an injury than even-keeled people. One instant decompression tactic: Take your dog on a run with you. Pets can help soothe stress.

68. Drink up. The simple loss of body water can decrease performance by more than 20 percent.

69. Cold out? Drink more. "Skiing is just like running track," says Miller. The difference: You're wearing a lot more clothes. Your body sweats during activity; if you can see your breath, you're venting moisture. Store a water bladder under your parka so it won't freeze.

70. Show up early at the golf course. Hit a bucket before your next round. "Most amateurs just show up late and rush to the first tee, take a practice swing, and play," Myers says. By gradually warming up for that first strike, you'll guard against incorrect body rotation on your takeaway—the primary cause of golf-related back injuries (and lost balls).

71. Check the lengths of your legs. When researchers at the University of Oulu, Finland, tracked 31 athletes for nearly 23 years, they discovered that 83 percent of those who experienced multiple fractures— that's several breaks that occur over time, not three at once—had different leg lengths. If you have pain in the hip, knee, or ankle, ask your doctor for a leg measurement during your annual physical. Some discrepancies can be solved with corrective insoles; many simply require strengthening hip flexors or loosening tight hamstrings.

72. Think about lingering concussions. In a study at the University of Toronto, researchers found that a concussion can cloud an athlete's judgment—and therefore his skills—for up to 21 days after the original bonk.

73. Avoid air-cell hell. Sidestep basketball shoes that have visible air cells in the heels. According to a study published in the *British Journal of Sports Medicine*, these shoes make you four times more likely to injure your ankles because of decreased heel stability. Try the Brand Jordan Team 10/16 ($110; www.jumpman23.com) instead. Its footbed is so low that it feels like a dress shoe.

74. Check your water losses. Weigh yourself before and after a long workout in

hot weather. If you've lost more than 3 pounds by the time you're finished, you're dehydrated and could be at risk of heatstroke. Invest in a water pack so you can easily sip throughout your workout. Hydrapak's Superfly model ($40, www.hydrapak.com) fits unobtrusively against the small of your back.

75. Eliminate fungus. Nail fungus is a serious—and sport-stopping—consequence of running. "Trauma to the toe caused by running can make the nail bed more susceptible to infection," says John Mozena, DPM, a marathon runner and a member of the Road Runners Club of America. "Sweaty socks are breeding grounds for fungi." Mitigate the mold-growing conditions with JoxSox ($7; www.joxsox.com). They're designed to wick away moisture and circulate air next to the skin, which frustrates fungi.

76. Before every swing, stretch. Try this before each golf shot: Grasp a club in both hands like a handlebar, hold it parallel to the ground, and lift it overhead. Bend forward at the waist with your shoulders as parallel to the ground as possible. With your arms extended, raise the club as far as you can overhead and behind you. It'll keep you from seizing up on the 18th, Mr. DiMarco.

77. Diagnose your trouble with a motion MRI. X-rays and scans show pictures of the problem area only while it's at rest. But dynamic kinematic MRI imaging, which enables patients to reproduce joint motion while being scanned, can pinpoint the spot in their range of motion at which the problem occurs. The technology works for the knees and ankles and is available at any hospital that has an open MRI.

78. Own the shoe that matches your game. Play tennis in tennis shoes. Unlike running shoes, which are made with an angled bottom to promote linear movement, tennis-shoe soles are flat for optimal side-to-side motion.

79. To strengthen, lengthen. Muscles that are strengthened as they lengthen can absorb more force, and this means less potential for tendon trouble. "It's called eccentric training," says Dr. Laskowski. Here's an ideal move for runners: In a calf raise, lift for 2 seconds, then spend 10 seconds lowering the weight. "The tissue is lengthening as it's contracting, and that trains it for force absorption and greater strength," he says.

80. Protect this joint. In a recent University of Iowa study, researchers examined young amateur athletes involved in contact sports—basketball, soccer, and wrestling—and found that wearing knee pads reduced the rate of lower-extremity injuries by 67 percent. Try Tru Fit pads ($13; www.thesportsauthority.com); even though their design covers the patella, they won't hinder play.

81. Sit up straight. "The number one reason people injure their backs is that they've developed muscular weakness," says Bert Fields, MD, director of Sports Medicine Fellowship at Moses Cone Hospital in

Hawk Soars After Surgery

You can't keep a good man down. Or, in some cases, even on the ground. That's why Tony Hawk found himself flying high above Mammoth Mountain in California a few years ago, riding his snowboard into big trouble. "After I took off, I realized I didn't have enough speed," the legendary skateboarder recalls. So instead of clearing the gap at the terrain park, Hawk landed hard. "I compressed my back knee too far as I tried to absorb the impact. I could tell something was wrong."

An MRI confirmed the diagnosis made by his orthopedic surgeon, David Chao, MD: meniscus and cartilage tears in his left knee. Within 48 hours of the injury, Hawk went under Dr. Chao's knife for a knee arthroscopy, trimming the tears and smoothing the cartilage.

Just 2 weeks post-op, Hawk was tracing big, flowing sine waves along his massive half-pipe ramp in Vista, California. It's the first time he had done so since his surgery, and Dr. Chao and Hawk's personal trainer, Barry Zeritzki, ATC, watched anxiously. Still, there's something miraculous in the amount of time elapsed between hurt and healed.

"It feels pretty good," announced Hawk as he slid to a stop at the base of the ramp. "The knee still feels a little weird, though."

Hawk rolled off the ramp and over to a folding table, where Dr. Chao put his hinge through slow, calculated movements. It's a healing touch Hawk trusts. After all, this doctor allowed him to fly once more.

Comeback Strategies

Aim small to jump big. As soon as Hawk came out of surgery, Dr. Chao had him hooked up to a knee-motion machine and began icing his knee. "You should start rehab from moment one," says Dr. Chao. "Set attainable goals, so you can see that you're achieving something."

Follow the 75-25 split rehab plan. Within 2 weeks, says Dr. Chao, you should be doing 75 percent functional and dynamic training—exercises that mimic the motions of your sport—and 25 percent resistance training. "Pumping on the ramp is basically a leg press for Tony's quads," says Dr. Chao.

Look for water. "For rehab, you can't beat swimming," says Barry Zeritzki, trainer for Hawk's Boom Boom Huck Jam Tour. Exercising in water allows for challenging cardiovascular endurance exercise long before you can safely do intense dryland training.

Greensboro, North Carolina. "[The weakness] leads to bad posture, and bad posture starts putting uneven weight or stress on the muscles, tendons, ligaments, disks, and vertebrae." Your first line of defense: a straight-shouldered stance.

82. Turn off the afterburners. Dr. Laskowski advises stretching after sustained activity. That's when bloodflow is higher in the muscles, which helps them benefit more from the stretch.

83. If you can't run with the big dogs, don't. Choose a league appropriate to your skill level. "Injuries tend to happen when things get out of control," says Robert Pedowitz, MD, PhD, chief of sports medicine services for the University of California at San Diego department of orthopedic surgery. Think of it this way: To borrow another animal-world metaphor, you'll be a big fish swimming in a small-pool relay lane and less likely to be swamped.

84. Squat, lunge, and step up. You'll reduce back and hamstring injuries by strengthening your glutes, or butt muscles. "Weak glutes force the hamstrings and lower back to compensate," says Micheal A. Clark, DPT, president of the National Academy of Sports Medicine. And because the hamstrings and back muscles are so long and produce so much force, they can bend your torso back like a plastic spoon. "Pretend you're squeezing a quarter between your butt cheeks to engage the glutes anytime your hip goes into extension," such as while stepping onto a box or lunging forward, Dr. Clark says.

85. Spend time relaxing in the mountains before your hike. Your exercising heart rate naturally adapts to high altitude, but you have to give it time, says David Pascoe, PhD, a professor of human performance at Auburn University. Training—or even sleeping—at high altitude accelerates this process. "You're also going to have a higher respiratory rate and lose more moisture," Dr. Pascoe says. So drink extra water, especially before and during hikes.

The 10 Most Common Sports Injuries

Our head-to-toe plan for winning the turf war

1. Neck pull: It's not an event in the World's Strongest Man competition, but rather a literal pain in the neck. When a sudden movement puts your neck in an awkward position, the muscles and ligaments that hold together the top bones in the spinal column can stretch—or tear. Here's how to avoid it:

Neck stretch: Stand and tuck your chin toward your chest. Place your left hand on your right ear and gently rotate your head toward your left nipple while moving your right shoulder blade back and down. Hold for 20 seconds, then repeat on the other side. Do two sets of this and all the other stretches in this section, except where noted.

Lying extension: Lie on your back with your knees bent. Place a small folded towel under the bump on the back of your head. Pretend a cable is pulling your head back behind you into the towel as you try to tuck your chin toward your chest. Do two sets of 12 to 15 repetitions of this and all the other exercises in this section, except where noted.

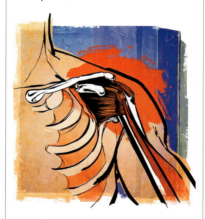

2. Shoulder impingement: Blame a weak rotator cuff, the group of muscles and tendons that tie the shoulder joint together. If your cuff is scrawny, repeatedly raising your arm can cause it to rub against the outer edge of your shoulder blade. Before you know it, the cuff will swell and become stuck under the blade. Here's how to avoid it:

Cuff stretch: Lie on your right side with your right upper arm against the floor and your elbow bent 90 degrees. Using your left hand, gently pull your right forearm down toward the floor until you feel a stretch in your right shoulder. Switch sides and repeat.

External rotation: Place a folded towel under your right armpit and stand so the outside of your left foot faces a cable station. Grab the middle handle with your right hand and rotate your arm horizontally to 2 o'clock. Rotate back. Turn around and repeat with your left hand.

3. Lumbar strain: Also known as "throwing your back out," a lumbar strain occurs when poorly conditioned muscles and ligaments in your

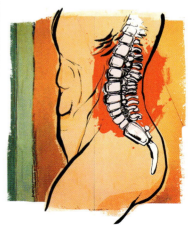

lower back are suddenly overworked. All it takes is a quick twist—especially while bending forward to, say, grab a ground ball. Here's how to avoid it:

Hip-flexor stretch: Stand with your right leg behind you as far as it can go while still keeping your feet flat on the floor. Turn your right foot inward slightly, then extend your right arm toward the ceiling. Draw your abs in and bend to the left. Repeat the move on the other side.

Lying foot slide: Lie on your back with your knees bent and feet flat on the floor. Draw your belly button toward your spine and slowly slide one foot forward as far as you can without allowing your back to arch. Return to the starting position, then slide the other foot forward and back.

4. Tennis elbow: Any activity in which you repeatedly twist your wrist or forearm—golf, racquetball, tennis—can damage the tendons that connect your hand to your

elbow. So why isn't it called "tennis hand"? The injury occurs at the elbow end. Here's how to avoid it:

Elbow stretch: Place the back of your right hand against a wall beside you, fingers pointing down. Tuck your chin and move your left ear toward your left shoulder. Hold for 2 seconds. Complete 10 repetitions, then press your palm against the wall and stretch again. Do the same routine with your left hand.

Cable wrist curl: Grab a low-pulley cable with your right hand, face the weights, and use your wrist to raise and lower the handle. Do this with your palm up, thumb up, and

palm down. That's one rep. Hit your left arm the same way.

5. Runner's knee: Every time your shoe strikes the ground, your knee feels it. Eventually, your kneecap may start to rub against your femur. The result: cartilage damage, inflammation, and tendinitis. Here's how to avoid it:

Biceps femoris stretch: Lie on your back. Pull one knee toward your chest, then across your body till it's lined up with your navel. Straighten the knee as far as you can, then flex your toes toward you. Hold for 2 seconds, then bring your knee back to your chest and repeat.

Tube walk: Stand and loop resistance tubing around your ankles. Sidestep 15 times to your right, then back to your left.

6. Pulled hamstring: The hamstrings and quadriceps work together to bend and straighten your legs. But when your quads become significantly stronger than your hamstrings, the hammies become fatigued and susceptible to strain as they try to "keep up." Here's how to avoid it:

Hip-flexor stretch: Stand with your right leg as far behind you as possible while keeping your feet flat on the floor. Turn your right foot in slightly, then extend your right arm toward the ceiling. Draw your abs in and bend to the left. Repeat the move with your left leg back and left arm raised.

Swiss-ball squat: Place a Swiss ball behind your back and up against a wall. With your weight against the ball, slowly lower your body until your thighs are parallel to the floor. Pause, then push yourself back up.

7. Achilles tendinitis: The Achilles' heel of your Achilles tendon is stiffness. If you don't stretch it properly, quick movements can inflame or even rupture it. Here's how to avoid it:

Soleus stretch: Stand in front of a wall with your feet hip-width apart and staggered. Bend your back knee 30 degrees, turn your back foot inward, and lean against the wall until you feel the stretch. Repeat with the other leg.

Inverted calf raise: Stand with one foot on a step and the other off the floor. Point your weight-bearing foot 45 degrees inward, rise onto your toes, and

slowly lower your weight until your heel goes below the level of the step. Repeat with the other foot.

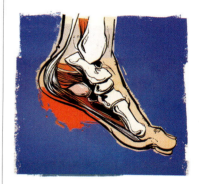

8. Plantar fasciitis: If you could look deep into your sole, you'd see the plantar fascia, the band of tissue that connects your heel bone to the ball of your foot. When this dual-purpose shock absorber and arch support is overworked, microtears develop, and you feel pain with every step. Here's how to avoid it:

Plantar stretch: From a seated position, place the palm of your hand over the toes of your foot and pull back until you feel a gentle stretch on the bottom of the foot. Repeat with the other foot.

Ankle scoop: Place a bench in front of the low pulley of a cable station. Sit with your legs straight and your ankles hanging off the edge of the bench, and wrap a pulley handle around your right foot. Flex the foot toward you and rotate it inward in a scooping motion, then return it to the starting position. Repeat with your left foot.

9. Shin splints: Because your shin muscles have to bear as much as six times your body weight during exercise, it's easy for foot-pounding activities to wear them down. Inflict enough abuse and the inflamed muscle can pull from the

bone. Here's how to avoid it:

Peroneal stretch: Stand in front of a wall with your feet staggered and hip-width apart. Move your back leg inward a few inches and point the foot at about a 45-degree angle toward your opposite heel. Lean against the wall until you feel a stretch in your calf.

Multiplanar hop: Standing on one foot, jump forward and land softly on the other foot. Then jump back to the starting position. Repeat out to the side and in again, then at a 45-degree angle backward, rotating so your foot points that direction, then back to the starting position.

10. Ankle sprain: Certain things, like dice, were designed to be rolled—but not your ankles. Best case: inflammation and mild pain. Worst: a complete tear that causes severe pain and swelling. Here's how to avoid it:

Peroneal stretch: Stand in front of a wall with your feet

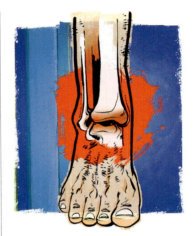

staggered and hip-width apart. Move your back leg inward a few inches and point the foot at about a 45-degree angle toward your opposite heel. Lean against the wall until you feel a stretch in your calf.

Balance reach: Stand on one foot on an Airex pad or a pillow and extend your other leg out in front of you, then bring it back. Next, extend the leg out to your side and back in again. Then extend it at a 45-degree angle backward, rotating it so your foot points in that direction, and return to the starting position.

BY DANIEL DUANE

Make the World Your Gym

The star of *Into the Blue* takes the work out of working out—and reaps the benefits

Watching women react to Paul Walker can be humbling.

The problem isn't so much the blushing teenage fans, but the adults, the ones you wouldn't mind meeting yourself. And to make matters more confusing, you actually do meet them when you spend a day with Walker, because his seeming disinterest and sheer Paul Walker-ness tend to keep women from approaching him directly. I learned this in the middle of a typical Paul Walker day, which involves spending maximum time getting serious exercise outdoors. We were standing on a concrete seawall near Oahu's Diamond Head peak, checking the waves below his nearby apartment, when this lovely woman appeared, fit and tan and wearing a tasteful little bikini, and started talking to me. She was in Hawaii on a job, she said, and was tired of hanging out with her coworkers. She was a surfer, and she wanted to know if we were going out in the water just then. And right when I started feeling pretty flattered about being the one getting all the female attention, Walker leaned over and whispered in my ear, "I'm kind of feeling that."

Then he did something remarkable: He simply took off his shirt.

Now, maybe he was just overheated in the tropical noon sun. And we were at the beach. Could've been purely innocent. But the effect of this one simple act was clear: Looking this naturally fit and fair had simply taught the guy that if he wanted someone's attention, all he had to do was create a diversion that would make her look at him. If she happened to see his bare torso in the process, well then, mission accomplished. And there was nothing arrogant or calculated about this. It was just common sense.

Which brings up an obvious question: How does a man get to look like Paul Walker? The face, of course, we can't help you with. And he doesn't have a nutritionist or a personal trainer we can refer you to. But there is a program, a very effective and simple one. "My motto is, you have to get in a sport a day," says Walker, who just turned 32. "Playing a little basketball, volleyball, going out surfing, skating, whatever it is. It's the best way to live." As for diet, "My mom was always really healthy and cautious about her diet, so I'm not a big sugar guy. But other than that, I just eat lean."

Walker tried weight lifting back when he was shooting *Varsity Blues*, in 1998. "I was surrounded by all these corn-fed football players," he says. "Everyone's like, 'Oh, you're going to be the action guy, you have to get bigger.' So I started this lifting program, and I'm taking creatine, and I got up to 205. Then I went on this surf trip to El Salvador." Not only did the extra muscle slow down his paddling, he says, but his endurance in the water wasn't as good. "I come back, and I'm down to 180, super-lean again, and I'm like, 'You know what? Hell with it. I'm done.' It's better for me to stay lean."

Nowadays, the only formal fitness training Walker does is martial arts, which strips unnecessary bulk off his frame while building his speed, balance, flexibility, and coordination. He starts every day with 2 hours of Brazilian jujitsu at a studio near his modest Santa Barbara home, then follows up with an hour of Muay Thai kickboxing. After that, it's all about the water: "If there's any surf, any fishing, I'll whip out in the boat." That would be the fast rigid-inflatable that allows Walker to rip across to the Channel Islands and catch a few waves, maybe spear a calico bass for dinner, then have a buddy drive while he surfs the boat wake all the way home. And if he's still itching for a good time after all that, he and some friends might do a few downhill skateboard runs on a quiet canyon road, or take his Nissan Skyline (0 to 60 in 5.2 seconds) to the racetrack. (Walker had professional race training when he starred in *The Fast and the Furious*,

and now he takes full advantage of his skills most weekends.)

All that fun serves to put a smile on Walker's face, sure, and gets him attention from bikini-clad surfer girls if he so desires, but it also gives him a kind of all-around fitness and toughness that comes in handy on the job. Shooting his new movie, *Into the Blue*, about four friends who discover treasure in a shipwreck, required relentless underwater work and long breath holds. Peter Zuccarini, who directed all the underwater photography, says, "At first, it was just Paul learning how to free dive, with Jessica Alba in a bikini, on a bright white sand bottom in beautiful warm water. They get sort of tender and intertwined, holding their breath, swimming along, doing dolphin undulations around each other—really graceful stuff. I think he was enjoying himself."

But later, Zuccarini shot a sequence in which Walker had to dive 60 feet without air tanks, then swim along the edge of a dropoff, where the coral suddenly falls 2,000 feet into an abyss. While the camera crew wore 7 millimeter wet suits against the cold, and chain mail against the omnipresent reef and tiger sharks, Walker wore nothing but board shorts. In the scene, his character is following a trail of airplane wreckage. "Every time he picked up a piece," Zuccarini says, "a shark would swim up, so he was having to do a long breath hold, pick up a part, react to it as an actor, and then deal with the fact that every time he picked up some scrap metal, a shark would come in to see if it might be food." Director John Stockwell (*Blue Crush*) says that what made it all possible was the hypercompetitive relationship that developed between Walker and costar Scott Caan. "When Scott showed some aptitude under-water as a breath holder and free diver, Paul was like, 'Okay, I'm going to go deeper and stay longer.' So they kept pushing each other."

Walker attributes his fighting spirit to his grandfather, a World War II veteran who also fought twice for the middleweight boxing title, and his father, who was in the Air Cavalry in Vietnam and fought a few ama-teur bouts. Walker grew up with a speed bag and a heavy bag in his family's backyard. His

dad taught him a lot of punch combinations, and he wanted to be like his forebears so much that when the first Gulf War broke out, he decided to enlist. The only reason he didn't actually go to war, he says now, is that "I went home bragging about the idea, thinking my dad would think it was cool, and he goes, 'You say that one more time, I'm going to knock your ass out, nail you in a crate, and ship you to Canada.'" His dad had seen enough of war to want his son's energy directed elsewhere.

Thus the surfing, an obsession that Walker sometimes places even above his fast-rising Hollywood career. Growing up in Sun Valley, California, Walker surfed every time his family went to the beach; these days he surfs almost every day. "It keeps things grounded for me," he says. "It's where I came from, and it's who I am. I sometimes strug-gle, because my job is like the antithesis of what surfing is all about. Surfing's simple. It's real."

We were out in the clear, blue Hawaiian water now, and a wave appeared on the horizon as Walker spoke. He spun to catch it. While he was gone, our female friend from the seawall paddled up to me on her own surfboard and struck up another con-versation. I assumed Walker would want to rejoin us—it was such an effortless and high-quality hookup—so when I finally caught his eye, I started waving.

Walker waved back, then pointed to the horizon: Another big wave was on the way, he meant to say, and shouldn't we try to catch it?

Get Out There!

These are the best adventure-sports schools and camps.

Whitewater Kayaking

Body benefit: "It looks as if the paddle stroke is all arms, but the power actually comes from your torso," says pro kayaker Ben Selznick. As a resistance exercise, paddling is unique in that it works both sides of your body while strengthening your core, which results in better posture and tighter abs. Kayaking also provides a modest cardio workout and improves focus.

Muscles used: Shoulders, back, arms, lower back, and abs

Calorie burn: 410 per hour

Where to learn: Otter Bar Lodge Kayak School, Forks of the Salmon, California. With top instructors and front-door access to class III and IV rapids, Otter Bar is the nation's premier kayak school. The 7-day, $1,950 course includes all gear, meals, and lodging. Open from mid-April to late September. 530-462-4772, www.otterbar.com

Scuba Diving

Body benefit: You won't break a sweat diving, but you'll burn calories, your upper body will get a workout hauling gear, and your lower body will see heavy action finning against currents. Plus, scuba is a mind-body relaxation exercise. "Underwater, there are no phones and no e-mails, plus you're weightless," says Travis Gainsley, of Pro Dive USA. "It has a Zen aspect."

Muscles used: Quads, hamstrings, calves, chest, and abs

Calorie burn: 574 per hour

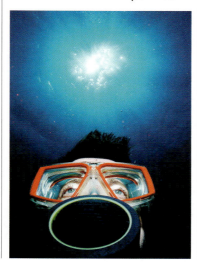

Where to learn: Pro Dive USA, Fort Lauderdale, Florida. Pro Dive is widely considered the world's top scuba training center. Though Pro Dive can fast-track you from novice all the way to dive master in just 2 months, the 4-day open-water certification ($375) will have you diving on reefs and shipwrecks within hours. 800-800-3483, www.prodiveusa.com

Snowboarding

Body benefit: On first thought, boarding doesn't seem like a workout—ride a lift up the mountain, slide back down. But, says Myra Foster, of Vermont's Stratton Mountain, "Your legs and hips are worked when you turn, and you use your abs to get up after you wipe out."

Muscles used: Hamstrings, quads, calves, abs, and ankles

Calorie burn: 574 per hour

Where to learn: Stratton Snowboard Camps, Stratton Mountain, Vermont. Besides regularly hosting the US Open of Snowboarding, Stratton Mountain opened its first board school in 1983 and today employs more than 50 instructors. Two-day clinics are offered from mid-November to mid-April for $340, which includes lodging. In March, Stratton offers a $450 3-day clinic taught by Olympic gold medalist Ross Powers. 802–297–4000, www.stratton.com

Mountain Biking

Body benefit: "A big part of the draw of mountain biking is that it's a fitness sport, an exploring sport, and a technical-skills sport, all in one," says former mountain-bike champ John Stamstad. Besides being a hell of a cardio workout, mountain biking improves balance, coordination, and reaction time.

Muscles used: Quads, calves, hamstrings, glutes, and hip flexors

Calorie burn: 697 per hour

Where to learn: Singletrack Ranch, Nationwide (Arizona,

Oregon, Utah, Vermont, West Virginia). Owned by John Stamstad himself, Singletrack specializes in improving the skills of intermediate and advanced bikers in epic destinations, such as Snowshoe, West Virginia, and Moab, Utah. The 3-day camps start at $900, which includes lodging, food, and personal attention from Stamstad. 206-650-6014, www.singletrack ranch.com

Surfing

Body benefit: "When you're a beginner, surfing is a total cardio and upper-body workout, because you're

constantly paddling out through the waves," says Izzy Paskowitz, a former pro long boarder and the current director at Paskowitz Surf Camp. Once you've learned to ride the waves back to shore, you'll develop core and leg strength and balance.

Muscles used: Arms, shoulders, back, abs, calves, and quads

Calorie burn: 246 per hour

Where to learn: Paskowitz Surf Camp, San Diego, California. Legendary within the surfing community, the Paskowitz family has been teaching beginners since 1972. Held June to September, Paskowitz Surf Camp's 6-day sessions include all-day instruction, equipment, food, and camping for $1,250 to $3,000. 949-728-1000, www.paskowitz.com

BY DOUG DONALDSON

Shift into High Gear

Six surefire strategies to improve your cycling

If you're interested in keeping your ego intact, don't ride your bicycle up a 4,784-foot mountain in a peloton of professional riders.

I came here to Georgia's Brasstown Bald in search of cycling tips, only to watch my form disintegrate on a 20 percent grade. Now I'm wobbling, bent over the handlebar as the pros recede in the distance. I suck in a deep breath and grunt forward. Five miles per hour will have to do.

I'm shadowing Floyd Landis, leader of the Phonak cycling team, as he prepares for the 650-mile, 6-day Tour de Georgia. He'll place third, beating former teammate Lance Armstrong during a time trial. But for now, he's hanging back, dissecting my saddle style. "You have to grind out the climbs," says Landis, 29, a member of two Tour de France champion teams. "It's not always easiest to muscle them out."

I drop onto my seat, find an easier gear, and pump. Sure enough, the mountain begins to drop behind me, and I'm soon over the summit, crouched and catlike, my bike silent as I push 50 mph down the back side. Before long, Landis, bored perhaps, revs it up and fades into the horizon. But his six tips, imparted during our ride, stick with me.

Go Full Circle

Stomp like Godzilla on your pedals and you'll sacrifice power. You want to pedal a complete circle. The motion should feel smooth, almost as if you're wiping mud off the bottom of your shoe. As a pedal gets close to the bottom of a stroke, engage your calf muscle and hamstring and pull down and back, toward the bottom of your back tire. When the pedal is just past the bottom, engage the front of your shin and your hip flexors to pull up on the pedal through the back stroke. "Some people prefer to point their toes; others keep them level," says Landis. "How you pedal when you're working really hard is your most efficient way."

Find the Beat

Landis's chunky hams are proof that all legs are not created equal. Techniques differ, too: Some riders can pump out power more efficiently by muscling through lower gears, while others are better at spinning fast. Your goal should be to find your highest comfortable cadence, or number of revolutions per minute (rpm). Lower cadences and tougher gears stress your joints and cause you to burn energy less efficiently, recover more slowly, and hit the wall faster as lactic acid builds up. "Most beginning riders spin too slowly," says Landis, adding that 90 rpm is a solid goal on flat ground. (Pros ride as high as 130.) Landis suggests this drill to find your ideal rate: Spin at 60 rpm for 2 minutes, then rev up to 110 for 2 minutes. Alternate for a total of 16 minutes, then ride at a steady speed at the highest comfortable rate you can maintain for 15 minutes. That's your ideal cadence.

Cut Corners

Turning is about shifting balance, not about twisting the handlebar. Do it right and you'll ease through turns with a dip of your shoulder. Do it wrong and you'll be shopping for the big box of Band-Aids. Trust your tires. "Ride on some wet grass and practice cornering," Landis says. "It'll teach you how to react when your bike starts to slide." On dry roads, reach your turn speed three or four lengths before the corner and keep your inside pedal up as you enter. Keep most of your weight on the outside (down) pedal.

Sit Out the Climbs

Standing on climbs might feel more powerful than staying seated, but it's not as efficient: A study in the *Canadian Journal of Applied Physiology* found that seated climb-

How to Fix Your Bike

Here are some simple cycle fixes.

Saddle height: When a pedal is at the bottom, your knee should be slightly bent. If your hips rock as you pedal, your seat is too high. If your heels drop as you pedal, the seat's too low.

Saddle tilt: A slight downward tilt relieves pressure on the front of your anatomy. Tilting the saddle slightly up will relieve pressure on sit bones. Find what's most comfortable for you.

Forward-backward saddle position: With your feet on the pedals and the crank arms level, the bump just below the kneecap of your forward leg should be over the pedal axle.

Arm reach: No Superman pose when reaching for your handlebar. Your elbows should be slightly bent when your hands are resting on the brake hoods. Swap the stem to adjust.

ers had a 6 percent lower heart rate over a 5 percent incline. Grind when you can, shifting into easier gears and upping your cadence. "I don't use my arms or other muscles, and I don't breathe as hard," says Landis, who takes 90 percent of hills—even in the Alps and Pyrenees—sitting down. "It just feels easiest, and after long races, my lower back doesn't get as sore."

When seated, keep your weight slightly back in the saddle and your hands loosely wrapped around the top of the bar (any lower decreases lung capacity). When your cadence drops below 65 rpm, or when you want to stretch or attack the hill, rise up. Keep your elbows in and your hands around the brake hoods. Your head should be above

One-Stop Bike Shop

Here are wheels to suit your style.

LeMond Alpe d'Huez: Old-school cred meets new technology in this racing stalwart, which sports a carbon-fiber seat stay and chainstays to absorb rough roads. It'll velvet-cushion your ride better than bikes twice its price, making it perfect for fast-paced cyclists looking for room to improve. ($1,650; www.lemondbikes.com)

Jamis Coda Sport: Meet your new morning commute. Unlike typical road bikes, the Coda has a flat handlebar and a more upright position so you can keep your head up as you surf traffic, and be more comfortable on long rides in the country. A suspension seatpost cushions your butt, and eyelets make it easy to add cargo racks for backpack-free transit. ($540; www.jamisbikes.com)

Trek 1000: Start here if you're just getting in the game: The 1000 has Shimano Sora and Tiagra components found on more expensive road bikes, and its triple chain ring gives beginners a larger choice of gears—especially in the lower, easier range. ($570 plus dealer fee; www.trekbikes.com)

the stem. Use your weight and your back and arms to pull yourself down; imagine you're stepping over 2-foot hurdles, pulling up on your foot as it nears the top of the arc.

Feel the Draft

When Landis's team pulled out an underdog victory in the 2004 Tour de France team time trial, their wheels were an inch apart. For mortals, 5 inches "will give you time to react if something goes wrong." Farther than 8 inches, there's little benefit. Start by tucking in about a foot behind the rider ahead. You'll hear a whoosh as you duck inside his or her airspace. Don't overlap wheels. If the wind is blowing from the right, move slightly to the left, and vice versa. Avoid braking; sit up to catch wind to adjust your speed.

Swoop Down Descents

One mistake on a downhill and you could end up gravel paste. "The most dangerous time for a descent is at the end of a day or end of a ride, when you're tired, because reaction times are slower," Landis says. Keep your weight back on the saddle and lower your upper body so it's parallel to the ground. "Some people lean even lower, but that means you have to crane your neck upward," he says. Ride with your hands in the drops—the curved sections of the handlebar—with your fingers over the brake levers. Landis and other pros pedal downhill; they have a finish line to get to. You should spin a little to keep lactic acid from pooling and making you stiff.

BY DAVID SCHIPPER

Shrink Your Handicap

Six tour-tested tricks to better your golf game

Todd Hamilton is not happy. I've just schooled the reigning British Open champ on our first hole at East Lake Golf Club in Atlanta. My first shot found the green; his hit the rough. I two-putted for par; he tapped in for a bogey.

I suppress the urge to pump the air, triumphant, but a grin slips out. Hamilton sees it, returns it, and raises me. "How about a hundred bucks on the next one?" he says, flush with motivation.

"Sure," I say. "Let's do it."

I've swung a few clubs over the years—I'm a 12 handicapper—but frankly, I'm not qualified to carry Hamilton's bag. As I step up to the next tee, I realize this, and my mind starts to race: You suck, Schipper. You haven't swung a club in months. You'd shank a basketball with a snow shovel. I squint, shuffle my feet, look down my forearms, and try to remind myself, *Keep your hands soft, arms straight, shoulders back, swing slow . . .*

Thwack! I watch my ball whirl, cockeyed, down the left side of the fairway. It lands in a hollow surrounded by some shaggy trees. Hamilton steps up, pauses, then uncoils. His ball rockets skyward, severing the blue Georgia sky. It falls toward the middle of the green and continues its graceful journey toward the pin.

"Nice shot," I manage.

Hamilton birdies the hole, I double-bogey. By the end, I lose big. But on one hole, I proved myself against a PGA pro—and milked him for a lesson, to boot. Six of his best tips follow.

Hey, Tiger, we still on for this weekend?

Stay on Track

Imagine a set of railroad tracks leading to the hole. "You want the clubface to be on the outer track and your feet, hips, and shoulders on the inner track," says Hamilton. If you're hitting with a 5-iron, keep the ball slightly ahead of center (toward your left foot if you're right-handed). The smaller the club number, the more you should move the ball forward on the track—with your driver, the ball should be almost at your left heel. With high-numbered clubs, move your ball back. Keep your knees flexed over your shoestrings as if you were about to complete a squat. Start your swing with your weight distributed evenly on each leg, but add more weight to your right when you take the club back. Throw this weight onto your left leg as you swing through the ball.

Grip with Your Fingers

Ever wonder why there are so many duffers around? "Most golfers don't grip the club correctly," says Hamilton. "They put the club in their palm, making it hard to snap through the ball. That leads to a slice." If you're right-handed, hold the club with your left fingers—position it directly over the point where your fingers meet your hand—pointing your thumb straight down the shaft. Lay your right hand over it so your right palm is over your left thumb. If you have short fingers, interlock your right pinkie with your left index finger; if you have longer fingers, overlap them. Make sure the V between your right thumb and index finger points directly up your arm to your

Turn on Your Power

A powerful rotational turn will give you an extra 10 yards off the tee or 10 mph on your fastball. Exercises to boost that strength are overlooked but important. "Most sports require stabilization, strength, and power through some type of rotation," says Tyler Wallace, NASM-CPT, of the National Academy of Sports Medicine. Here are the exercises Wallace recommends for powering up some key sports moves.

Golf swing: Stability ball Russian twist

Lie with your shoulder blades and head on a stability ball and your feet flat on the floor. Hold your arms straight above you and clasp your hands together. Slowly rotate your shoulders to the left until your arms are roughly parallel to the floor. Pause, then rotate to the right. Do two sets of 15 repetitions.

Baseball swing: Standing cable rotation

Stand between the weight stacks of a cable station. Grab both ends of a rope handle attached to the midlevel pulley. Keeping your elbows bent, rotate your body to the left. Pause, then return to the starting position. Do three sets of 10 reps on each side.

Tennis stroke: Standing medicine-ball rotation chop

Hold a medicine ball overhead with your arms straight. Keeping them straight, swing your arms down as if to throw the ball to the outside of each foot. Do four sets of eight repetitions on each side.

Hockey slap shot: Single-arm stability-ball rotation row

Grab a dumbbell and lie facedown on a stability ball. With the weight in your right hand, let your right arm hang down. Place your other hand on your hip. Pull the weight up toward your chest as you rotate your upper body to the right. Pause, then slowly return to the starting position. Do two sets of 15 with each arm.

Baseball pitch: Medicine-ball lift

Lift a medicine ball from your chest to above your shoulder, rotating your hips and pivoting your back foot as you go. Pause when your arms are straight, then lower the ball. Do three sets of 10 reps on both sides.

Green Giants

Contrary to marketing hype, there's no one golf ball that fits all. We tested the latest crop to find the right ball for every game (and wallet).

Wilson Staff Px3, $25 a dozen

The hype: Shallow dimples rip through the air to create a more stable flight, while a "performance mantle" inside means more spin so it sticks to the green. A urethane elastomer cover improves control around the green.

The reality: It flew true and felt great off the clubhead. The best part: no buyer's remorse when we lost one. It's perfect for performance-driven golfers who take chances around the green.

Nike Mojo, $28 a dozen

The hype: It's described as the next-generation distance ball, promising maximum travel with minimum compression for a smoother feel.

The reality: It played well without hitting the wallet hard. The acid-inspired packaging and engraved MOJO lettering are enough to keep most hacks entertained. Overall, a great all-purpose ball for the high-handicapper out for a weekend round.

Callaway HX Hot, $40 a dozen

The hype: The reinforced ionomer cover produces a "hot" ball that jumps off the clubface. Hexagonal dimples, not round ones, cut through the wind.

The reality: It went the distance but had a rocklike feel to it. Play it if you're a short hitter looking to add length, or a big hitter looking to reach Russia. Great for longer, more modern courses that require less touch and more launch.

Nike One Black, $54 a dozen

The hype: It has the biggest core Nike engineers have ever created, for a more efficient transfer of energy at contact and, thus, longer distance.

The reality: It keeps spin rates low for more accuracy off the tee. The downside: It'll challenge the short game of most duffers, because imparting a greens-stopping spin on the ball means hitting it hard—harder than most weekend players are capable of.

Titleist Pro V1x, $58 a dozen

The hype: A speed-enhancing, spin-controlling ionomer casing improves control of full-iron shots.

The reality: It's widely used on the PGA Tour for good reason. But once again, as a low-spin ball, it's for the better player. If you're not shooting in the mid-80s, don't bother. Instead, try the Titleist NXT ($36 a dozen), which uses a hacker-friendly version of the technology.

right shoulder. Finally, and most important: Don't grip it too tightly. "Sam Snead always thought of it like an open tube of toothpaste," says Hamilton. "Try not to squeeze any out."

Find Your Trigger

Great golf swings look like one fluid motion, but they're made up of three components. First is the trigger. "It's hard to unfold such a complex movement from a complete standstill," Hamilton says, adding that he pushes his left foot into the ground to get him going. You can try that, or press the club handle with your index finger, or do whatever works for you—as long as it doesn't throw off your form. The other two components each have two movements. Recite the words *I'm a . . . golfer* while you swing. The first two words represent the pace of the backswing; the third, the downswing and follow-through. "If you bring the club back too quickly, it's going to fall off the tracks and mess up your downswing," says Hamilton. "But if you take it back nice and relaxed, you've won half the battle." The rest is basics: Keep your arms at your sides as if you were holding towels under your arms, form a neat triangle from your shoulders to the grip, and bring your clubhead back only as far as your left hand will go without overstretching. Let your knees slide forward to begin the downswing. Swivel your hips as you follow through. "Your belt buckle should point slightly in front of the ball at impact," says Hamilton.

Try Four Play

Ben Hogan, winner of four U.S. Opens and two Masters, once said the secret to putting is to "grab your wedge." In other words, if you chip well, you won't need to sink a 6-footer for par; you can just tap it in. "Divide the length of your chip into fourths," advises Hamilton. "Carry the ball a fourth of the distance, and it'll roll the rest."

Break the Rules

Once you make the green, start your putt by reading the break. Your secret signal: the cup. "Unless you're playing very early in the day, one side of the cup will look as if it's been used more," says Hamilton. "That's because all the balls are breaking into that side." Other tips: Shiny grass means you're down-grain, so the balls will break fast in the direction of the grass; dark green means you're hitting against the grain, so your putts will be slower.

Bowl for Birdies

Now it's time to putt. Imagine arrows leading to the hole like the ones on a bowling lane. "For a 15-foot putt, pick a spot that's one grip-length ahead of the ball," says Hamilton. And remember the railroad tracks: "Your feet are parallel to the inside track, and your putter goes back and through on the outside track." The ball should be just right of your left heel (the reverse for lefties). Swing with your shoulders and arms, not your wrists. "You want your wrists to be one with the stroke," says Hamilton.

BY MATT BEAN

Paddle Your Way to an Eight-Pack

Follow this seven-step plan to leave everyone in your wake

We're giving it to you straight: You're never going to swim like Michael Phelps. For starters, you're probably not 6'4"—and in the water, length means speed. Then there's your—by comparison—penguinlike wingspan. Phelps's span is 79 inches, and it propels him through the water like a nitro-fueled speedboat. And the 45 miles of practice he puts in a week? Great for him, but you have commitments.

Now, the good news: All of this had less to do with Phelps's six gold medals and three world records at the 2004 Olympics than one basic in-pool principle that anybody can learn: "The longer and more streamlined you can make your body, the faster you'll go," he says. "It's that simple."

Phelps and swimming guru Terry Laughlin, president of the New York–based swimming think tank Total Immersion (www.totalimmersion.net), helped us put together a step-by-step guide to leaving your lanemates behind. If you're a beginner, our plan will keep you from flailing about like you're being attacked by piranhas. If you're a pro, we'll show you how to shave seconds without having to shave your knees.

We're focusing on the freestyle stroke here, not only because it provides a killer cardio workout, but also because it works the most muscles overall—building core strength and carving your V. And it shreds calories. Blows them right out of the water, in fact. Phelps is as thin as an Olsen twin, yet he eats 8,000 calories a day. His average breakfast: two egg-and-cheese sandwiches, a bowl of grits, a western omelet, French toast, and a stack of chocolate-chip pancakes ("for dessert," he says). Being 19 doesn't hurt, of course, but if Phelps can keep his abs well groomed despite eating enough for four, you should be able to make sizable strides with just a modest amount of effort.

Here's how to maximize nature's perfect exercise.

Swim Tall

"Water is 1,000 times denser than air," says Laughlin. "So the single most important factor is to slip your body through the smallest hole in the water." Imagine a central axis extending from the top of your head to the opposite end of the pool. Rotate your body along this axis with each stroke, stretching your leading arm (the one reaching out front) as far forward as you can. Keep the muscles in your lower back and abs taut as you power through the water. Doing so will keep the propulsion coming from both your arms and legs and stop your midsection from sagging like an old first-mate's belly.

Drop an Anchor

Swimming with just your hands is like jumping with just your feet. Instead, grip the water with your entire forearm and hand, holding your forearm at a right angle to your upper arm and digging in like you're gathering sand with a shovel. Keep your hands broad, flat, and firm. You're not pushing your arm through the water as much as anchoring it and pulling your body over it.

The Start

The glide phase of a racing dive is the fastest you'll ever travel through the water. Here's how to blow anyone off the block.

The countdown: Start like a sprinter on a diving block or the edge of a pool. Curl the toes of your forward foot over the edge of the block, with the toes of your dominant foot several inches behind the front heel. Grab the edge of the block with your hands spread shoulder-width apart. Lean forward slightly, using your arms for balance.

The launch: Explode out and up like a javelin. Keep your body tight and maintain height for as long as possible. Your head should be down, arms extended, hands locked together, with one hand on top of the other, and your biceps should squeeze your head right above your ears. Press your legs together, point your toes, and generally try your best to resemble a ballistic missile.

The splashdown: "When I hit the water," says Michael Phelps, "I just try to keep my body really tense so I enter as cleanly as possible." Your goal is to make a single-hole, splashless entry.

Put Yourself on Heavy Rotation

Each stroke begins with your leading arm having entered the water, and that side of your body—the low side—pointing almost at the bottom of the pool. The other side of your body—the high side—should be raised, with the arm that just finished its stroke getting ready to return to the water. Power is triggered when you drive down the high side of your body, Laughlin says, throwing your high-side arm forward along the central axis into the leading position and forcefully rotating your hips and torso. Meanwhile, your low-side arm becomes the pulling arm underwater, working with your rotating torso to provide acceleration.

Keep Your Head Down

Freestylers used to hold their heads high. That forced the rest of the body to drop, turning it into a high-drag plow. "I look pretty much straight down at the bottom of the pool," says Phelps. Not only does this technique cut drag, it keeps your torso high, reducing strain on your neck and lower back.

Find Your Glide Path

In the pool, fewer strokes is better. Your goal should be a high DPS—swim-speak for "distance per stroke." Elite swimmers like Phelps can easily traverse a 25-yard pool in seven strokes (each hand entry counts as a stroke). Try to keep yours below 20 by conserving momentum. Pull yourself over your anchor and continue to glide forward with one arm forward and the other back. "You'll travel farther and faster with your legs

streamlined near your axis," says Laughlin. When you begin to slow, start the next stroke.

Drag Your Feet

"If you're a good kicker, you're a good swimmer," says Phelps. The secret is turning your feet into fins. Here again, leverage rules: Your legs should be taut, scissoring you through the water, while your feet remain flexible. This will help them snap at the downstroke of each kick, adding oomph and helping twist your torso along the central axis. If your feet don't flex well, buy a set of kicking fins (we like the Slim Fin; www.forcefin.com) to add flexibility.

Don't Waste Your Breath

Gasping for air every time your head nears the surface is a great way to drown. Instead, make each breath count. Emphatically exhale the air from your lungs (all of it, not just 90 percent) before snagging a quick, full breath on the high side. Beginning swimmers need to breathe after each stroke, but as your endurance improves, try breathing on alternate sides—that is, after three strokes. It'll reduce the strain on your neck and shoulders that results from always breathing on the same side.

The Perfect Stroke

Olympic swimming coach Terry Laughlin analyzes thousands of strokes each year. The key to an efficient freestyle stroke, he says, is keeping your body as close to its central axis as possible. Here's how.

Step 1: Your power stroke starts here, with your right arm about to begin the pulling phase, your right leg ready to kick, your left hip ready to drop, and your left arm poised to reenter the water after the stroke.

Step 2: This is your horsepower phase. Set your right hand and forearm like an anchor in the water and let your back and torso muscles rotate your body past it. Your left hip drops along the central axis, transferring power through your core to the pulling arm. Meanwhile, your left arm is stretched out in front, lengthening your body and helping force down your high side to add torque to your torso and hips. "That rotation releases far more energy than you have in your arm muscles," says Laughlin. Continue pulling yourself over your anchored arm—beginners often lay off the gas at this point—almost as if you were trying to push water out of the pool above your hip.

Step 3: Keep your thighs a few inches apart and within the slipstream envelope your torso creates as it pushes through the water. Keep your legs as straight as possible and your ankles loose, with your feet acting like fins. The downbeat of your left foot helps cock the left side of your body upward for the next stroke. By the end of your stroke, your left side is facing the bottom, with your right arm ready to return to the resting phase and your left prepared to begin a power stroke.

BY LIESA GOINS

Be the Best in Snow

Six slick slope tricks to get you
from bunny hill to black diamond

Freshman snowboarders share a common appreciation by the end of the first day: the high tensile strength of their tailbones. But it doesn't have to be that way, says veteran bruise-bearer Jake Burton, founder of Burton Snowboards. "A snowboard is made to respond to your inputs," he says. "The sooner you learn to quit fighting it, the sooner you'll quit falling."

Sadly, there's no way to completely erase the learning curve: No matter how athletic you are, your backside will sport some degree of black and blue by the time you find your snow legs. But you can speed your progress substantially. We asked a distinguished panel of powder experts, including Burton, for their shortcuts around Pain Mountain. Pay attention, or pay with your ass.

Lose a Leg

Since snowboard training wheels don't exist, try the next-best thing: logging one-legged practice time on a level surface, says Jeff Boliba, global resort manager for Burton

Essential Skill: Getting Off

Exiting a chairlift on a snowboard is harder than it looks. Let the chair do the work: As your butt leaves the seat, rest your back foot (it should be free) in the middle of the board. Bend your knees slightly, keep your spine upright, and point your board ahead. Wait for the chair to push you and coast straight forward, leaning back slightly on your heels. Step back with your back foot to stop. Bask in the applause, even if it's your own.

Snowboards Learn to Ride program. "It's called skating," he says. "Latch your front foot into the binding, but leave your back foot free to push. Not only is this useful for moving around on flat surfaces, but you'll develop a better sense of how to balance on a board."

Here's the trick: Lean on your front foot, but keep your balance centered in the middle of the board. Keep your weight in the arches of your feet, rather than on your heels or toes. It'll be easier to keep the board flat and stay off the edges, which can catch in the snow and land you headfirst in the fluff.

Shift Gears

Gravity's your gas on a snowboard, but there are right and wrong ways to accelerate off the line. Consider your front leg to be first gear, your back leg overdrive. As you start from a standstill, lean on the front leg to start moving (rock back and forth if you're rooted in place), then ease into a balanced position once you get going. Leaning on your back leg too much is like punching the gas in a funny car: Your front end will lift off the ground, and you'll lose control of where you're headed. Which means you'll probably be headed for the sturdy, unforgiving broadside of a tree somewhere.

Brake Up

Slowing down without sitting down is one of the toughest skills to nail. Here's the key: Apply pressure to whatever edge of the board is uphill, dragging yourself against the slope like a knife shaving butter. Your knees

Turn Tricks

Check out these 3 slope-shredding shortcuts.

The rails: Your baby steps start here. Scout out a beginner-friendly terrain park with boxes or rails close to the ground. Pick one, then stay low as you approach the rail. Lift your board off the ground (nose first, then tail) and swivel your hips until you glide onto the rail, straddling it. Keep your balance as you slide along, and let your momentum carry you back onto the ground. As you leave the rail, twist your hips to point the board back in the direction of travel. Bend your knees to absorb the landing.

The jumps: Start with a small jump, or kicker. Your approach is crucial; watch how other boarders pick a line. When it's your turn, point your board straight downhill and focus on where you want to land. "As long as you're centered, you can stick a landing," says half-pipe master and X-Games medalist Keir Dillon. Keep your board flat as you approach the lip and let your speed carry you forward; you don't actually need to push off. Track your landing spot while keeping your eyes down the slope and land evenly on both feet with the whole board.

The half-pipe: Once you're able to make it down the mountain without eating your weight in powder, consider taking on the half-pipe. Beforehand, you'll want to add 5 degrees of forward lean and turn both bindings 15 degrees toward the board's nose. Fall gently into the pipe—angling your board 45 degrees downhill—and chart an S-shaped path down the bowl, pumping back and forth between the

rims as you go. "The key is to not stand up," Dillon says. "Stay low for balance and let your legs cushion the impact of landing."

should be slightly bent, with your body angled slightly uphill to maintain your center of gravity. The same technique will help you regulate speed between turns.

Forget the Mountain

"Your instinct is to look down at your feet," says Adam Kisiel, ride-school supervisor at Breckenridge Resort. "Instead, look in the direction you want to slide." Turning your head will cause a natural weight shift, which will orient the board in the right direction. Also, look across the mountain, not downhill. You'll keep your feet, knees, hips, and shoulders aligned better, simplifying turns and preventing an unexpected

Dressed to Thrill

Turn that mountain into a molehill.

Burton Jeremy Jones snowboard: Multipurpose boards can handle powder and groomed trails alike. This one flexes slightly between the bindings for ultraresponsive handling and sports reinforced sidewalls to deal with whatever the mountain dishes out. ($500; www.burton.com)

Giro Fuse audio helmet: Helmets are smart. This one is genius. An integrated sound system lets you blast MP3s through headphones mounted in the insulated ear pads. We like James Brown's "Get Up." ($180; www.giro.com)

Ride Team binding: Bindings provide the steering control for your rig. The wrong pair and you'll be as agile as a 1972 Cadillac. These have carbon rebound rods, which means they're ultralight and handle like a Porsche. ($275; www.ridesnowboards.com)

Smith Prodigy goggles: Fog-free goggles have fallen flat for years. This is the first pair to truly make good on its clear-vision promise, thanks to a built-in battery-powered fan. ($180; www.smithsport.com)

K2 Proof boot: Bad boots are deal breakers. These let you fine-tune your fit using a dial, so you won't have to sacrifice your fingers for a snug fit. ($290 to $330; www. k2snowboards.com)

increase in speed. "It's a simple fix with huge benefits," says Mikey Franco, snowboard training coordinator at Jackson Hole Mountain Resort.

Turn Like a Cowboy

Posture's the hardest thing to master on a board, but it's impossible to carve without the right stance. The proper position is almost cowboylike, knees akim-bo and legs open. "Locking your legs or bending at the waist throws your balance in the wrong place," says Kisiel. Instead, hold your body as you would during squats—knees soft and upper body upright. The motion and movement for turning the board should then come from your hips down. "If you steer with your shoulders, you have to use much more effort," says Kisiel. "Toe-side" turns bring you face-first toward the hill, while "heel-side" turns leave you facing outward. In both cases, you'll grab the slope with the uphill edge of your board, using light but firm pressure from your toes or heels to broker the turn.

Bridge the Gap

Connecting toe-side and heel-side turns is the final step toward full-on carving. As soon as you complete one turn, lean gradually and gently toward the other edge. Use your hips to bring your board around and let your downward momentum pull you through the turn. Success hangs on your balance: Your weight should always remain centered on the board from left to right, but your balance toward and away from the slope. That's what glues the turns together.

BY MARK ANDERS

Catch a Wave

Five sure fire ways to keep
from falling over board

Paddling out to a wave with Kelly Slater is like bringing Shaq to your half-court pickup game. People stare. Some bow. A few manage a hello. But mostly they shut up and watch.

I meet up with the six-time world champion at the legendary Salt Creek break near Laguna Beach, California. The waves here are lightning quick, with hollow barrels wide enough for a Harley or two. Slater pounces on the first one that comes by, shredding it like Mark McGwire's credibility. Necks crane, following Slater as he paddles back beside me, and then everyone eyes the interloper—the guy on their turf who isn't an ambassador of the sport they all love and cherish, the guy who didn't shoot ads for Calvin Klein, the guy who never dated Pamela Anderson.

A shoulder-high wave rolls in, and, overcome by performance anxiety, I start stroking wildly.

I pop to my feet, but the bottom falls out. As I flail about, trying to regain my balance, Slater takes two quick strokes and drops in beside me. He's framed by the falling water as he threads a thin line through the barrel. He's soft but strong and fluid through the waves. I'm fluid-challenged. The wave crashes onto my head, sending me face-first into the waist-deep water. "Take off a little earlier," Slater says as I try to shake it off (the fall and the humiliation). "Once you line up with the wave, take longer and more deliberate strokes to get into it."

I nod and head off again. Sure enough, I nail the next wave. Over the course of the day, Slater gives me dozens of tips. Other surfers eavesdrop. You can, too. Here's what I learned.

Count 10 Before You Hang 10

Paddling is the most physically demanding part of surfing, and it can make or break your run. Your goal is to develop momentum before the wave sweeps underneath you and let it launch you into a standing position. Time your start so that you make at least 10 strong paddles before the wave's peak reaches you. Use long, fluid strokes, grabbing the water beneath your board with your hands cupped and your forearms almost perpendicular to the board. "Stay relaxed," Slater says, "using short little strokes to angle your board along the face of the wave." Keep your head up and the board flush with the waterline. "If the nose of the board is going under, you're too far forward," Slater says. Likewise, if the nose is pushing water as you paddle, you're too far back.

Essential Skill: The Duck Dive

Paddling out to surfable waves sometimes means getting past a series of less worthy whitecaps. The duck dive helps you slip underneath. When you're about 8 feet from an oncoming wave, grab your board on both sides and push up onto your knees with your butt in the air. Throw your weight forward as you rise, kicking one of your legs up with your knee bent at 90 degrees for a boost. Force the nose of your board down and under the wave. You'll slide under unscathed, too.

Use the Wave as a Trampoline

Once the wave is underfoot, let its energy propel you into a standing position. "Practice on the beach," suggests Slater. Draw an outline of a surfboard in the sand. From a prone position, explode off the ground, using equal force from your hands and feet. If you're regular-footed, your left foot should end up near the nose of the board, your right foot back. It's vice versa if you're goofy-footed. (Experiment to find which is more comfortable.) Be as smooth and quick as possible, doing five sets of 20 reps. Dry-land training is great for experienced surfers, too, improving their quickness and balance.

Surfing the Turf

A great wave is a terrible thing to waste. Here's how to know where to wait.

The soup: Also known as "the inside," this is the spot where the waves have already broken and are moving toward the beach in a mass of roiling whitewater. Learn the pop-up here if you're just getting started.

The peak: This is where the wave reaches its highest point and starts to break. Sit here to catch as many waves as possible. Understand the etiquette, though: The surfer closest to the break goes first. Drop in ahead of someone and you'll be asked to leave. Also, the most experienced surfers get to pick their waves. If you don't know who's the most experienced, it's not you.

The impact zone: This is no-man's-land, the spot between the soup and the peak. It's also the most dangerous place to find yourself, because it's where the waves unload the majority of their power.

The shoulder: It's the unbroken part of the wave, to the left or right of the peak. It's also a great spot for beginners and intermediates. They can practice in calmer waves. Just make sure you yield to surfers who are already up and riding the wave from the peak zone.

The outside: Located beyond the peak zone, it's where the big kahunas break. Patience is key; they're few and far between.

The channel: This is the safest and easiest route to paddle out to the peak. Look for an area of darker-colored water. Because the water's deep, fewer waves break here.

Move to the Center

Surfing is like politics: Take a stance too far left or right and you'll fall hard. Center your feet over the board's stringer (or center-line), straddling it with the arches of your feet. Your toes should be pointed directly toward the side of the board, your feet just slightly more than shoulder-width apart.

Corner at High Speed

As you start moving down the wave, you'll feel the bottom drop out. Just then, throw your weight forward onto your front leg to generate enough speed for turning. As you reach the lower part of the wave, step on the tail to lighten the load on the nose, and then turn into the wave. "As you initiate the turn, your front leg should be straight," says Slater. "As you finish the turn, your back leg should be straight and your front leg slightly bent."

Embrace Failure

"Never just wipe out," Slater says. "Be an active faller." Always try to put distance between you and your board, lest it smack you upside the head and render you unconscious. Kick it away or, at the very least, cover your head. Also, tumble toward the wave's shoulder, the part that hasn't broken yet. Avoid landing under the lip—the falling curtain of water that packs the majority of a wave's punch. Most important, never dive off your board headfirst. You could nail the bottom and really mess yourself up.

How to Catch a Wave

Kelly Slater shows you the way, step by drenching step.

1. As the wave approaches, lie down on the board and start paddling toward shore. Use strong, smooth strokes and keep your board perpendicular to the wave, but pointed slightly in the direction you hope to go.

2. As soon as you feel the wave start to pick you up, push down on the rails of the board just below your chest and, in one swift motion, pop up to your feet. Never go to your knees first.

3. Stand sideways on the board with your feet shoulder-width apart and knees slightly bent. Make sure your back foot is over your fins—the rudders underneath the board. Your front foot should be just under your chest and pointing forward.

4. Now, aim the board toward the shoulder—the smooth, open face of the wave—and let the wave push you there.

The Board Room

There's a stick to suit every surfer.

Buy this if you're a beginner: Edgecore Surf Joe Blair Speed Egg. The fins are 2 inches farther off the tail than those of the other boards here, allowing for tight but controlled turning. The extra-soft side rails and tail, meanwhile, reduce drag, making the board quick and smooth as well—a perfect combo for beginners. ($625; www.edgecoresurf.com)

Buy this if you want to cruise: Hobie Classic. This 9½-foot single-fin longboard is wide and stable, gliding like a pontoon. Surfing icon Hobie Alter added four redwood stringers for strength. ($950; www.hobie.com)

Buy this if you're chasing the big one: Rusty Cali-Gun. So-called gun boards—one part longboard, one part carver—have narrow, spearlike shapes for catching large, powerful waves. This one is stable for handling giant chop and nimble for steering clear of trouble. ($525; www.rusty.com)

Buy this if you want to carve: Channel Islands Flyer II. Pros love shortboards like this 6-plus-footer. The curvy outline and swallowtail carve fast and powerful surf, a tri-fin thruster adds speed and maneuverability, and the full rails below provide ample flotation on smaller waves. ($550; www.cisurfboards.com)

Raise Your Game

BY MIKE MEJIA, MS, CSCS

This workout will have you leaping and chopping in the gym, adding balance, coordination, and power to typical workout routines, and improving sports performance outside the gym. Do it 3 days a week, with at least 1 day of rest between. Do three sets of each exercise with 1 minute of rest between sets.

Unilateral hang clean: This is a multipart sequence that's meant to be executed quickly and powerfully.

Stand in a quarter squat, holding a dumbbell at knee level with one hand.

With your chest up and your back arched, rise on the balls of your feet as if you were about to jump. Simultaneously shrug the dumbbell upward as you pull it up with your arm.

Once the weight is at about chest height, dip under it by bending your knees and hips to "catch" the weight in front of your shoulder. The weight should roll to your fingers, with your wrist bent back and your upper arm parallel to the floor. Lower the weight and repeat for four to six repetitions, then do four to six reps with the weight in your other hand.

Split jump: Stand in a lunge position with one leg 2½ to 3 feet in front of the other, your arms at your sides. Bend at the knees until your back leg almost touches the floor.

Swing your arms forward and jump as high as you can. While in the air, switch leg positions so that you land softly with the other leg in front. Repeat for 8 to 12 repetitions.

Reverse woodchopper: Stand with your feet shoulder-width apart and hold a dumbbell with a hand-over-hand grip. Reach across your body so the dumbbell is to the outside of your left calf.

Now use your legs and core to swing the weight up over your right shoulder. Return to the starting position and do five to seven repetitions. Then swing the weight over your left shoulder for 5 to 7 more reps.

Training Tips

What's a good exercise to improve my golf swing?

Try the twister. "The golf swing is all about rotation," says Houston-based trainer Carter Hays, CSCS. "A golfer has to rotate virtually every joint to its functional capacity if he wants to come close to his potential." This exercise will help you rotate with more strength and through a greater range of motion at the hips and shoulders. Focus on initiating the move from your hips while keeping the rest of your body stable. Perform three sets of 12 repetitions, 3 days a week.

Twister: Get into a modified pushup position with your shins on a stability ball and your hands on the floor, directly beneath your shoulders. Slide your legs about halfway down the sides of the ball. Keeping your legs straight and your navel pulled in toward your spine, move the ball to the left by attempting to touch your left foot to the floor. Next, try to touch your right foot to the floor so the ball moves to the right and return to the starting position. That's one repetition.

What's the best thing to eat before a long bike ride?

Honey. Real honey breaks down more slowly in the body than other sugars, so it provides a longer-lasting energy supply, according to a study at the University of Memphis Exercise and Sports Nutrition Laboratory. Dive into your bag for a Honey Stinger Rocket Chocolate bar—one of the few nationally available energy bars made with real honey—or eat about 1 tablespoon of honey, says Richard Kreider, PhD, who led the research.

Is there one foolproof tip that'll help me correct my golf slice?

Absolutely. But first you have to understand why it's happening. "At the moment of impact, your clubface is pointing to the right [assuming you're a righty]," explains Laird Small, director of the Pebble Beach Golf Academy in California. This gives the ball a clockwise spin and causes it to shoot off to the right. (If your clubface were to point left at impact, the ball would spin counterclockwise and hook.) To correct your slice and avoid a hook, you need to hit the ball with a squared clubface. Do this by loosening your grip and allowing your arms to roll through the shot.

Here's an exercise that will give you a feel for that "crossover": Take the club in your left hand and, holding the upper half of that arm firmly against your side, swing the club back and through the ball. Your left arm should move only at the elbow joint. This will force you to roll your arm through the shot and impart some straight-flying backspin to the ball.

How do I hit a curveball?

Keep your focus and form, says Jim Romeo, a Louisville Slugger Coach of the Year who now trains hundreds of big-league hopefuls as director of the Spartans Sports Camp in Norwood, New Jersey. By identifying the pitch as it's thrown, you can adjust your swing accordingly.

1. Before the windup, focus on the pitcher's belt buckle or the front of his hat. As he begins his delivery, pan your eyes from the buckle or hat to the ball's release from the pitcher's hand. This eye movement keeps a batter's eyes relaxed and fresh to focus on the ball as it's released.

2. Keep your weight on your back foot, so you have a longer time to recognize the type of pitch and see the ball coming toward you. "Most people are looking for a fastball, so they lunge too early from their back foot to their front to hit the ball," says Romeo.

3. Recognize the pitch: When it leaves the pitcher's hand, a curveball will be rotating from top to bottom, like from 12 o'clock to 6 o'clock. The ball appears to leave the hand higher than a fastball; to the batter, it looks as if the ball is releasing above the pitcher's hand.

4. Swing away!

My college coach told me bench-pressing would ruin my hoops game. Was he right?

Bench-pressing has suffered a reputation for wrecking shoulders and jump shots, but we place the blame more on the exerciser than the exercise itself. Lifters hurt themselves when they use poor form or too much weight or when they don't balance their benching with exercises for other upper-body muscles. To stay safe, limit your bench-pressing to twice a week

and use a weight that you can manage without compromising good form. And balance your chest work by exercising your lats with an equal number of chinups or rows.

I'm starting to get into adventure sports. How long before a major trip should I start doing specialized workouts?

You'll need about 7 weeks of training if you're planning a grueling trip. Spend the first 3 weeks increasing the number of days per week that you've been training and build up to four sets of eight to 10 repetitions with unilateral movements—exercises that work each limb individually. Then take half a week off. Over the subsequent 3 weeks, add more core-strengthening exercises and plyometrics to your workout. Take another 3 to 4 days off to let your body recover so you can start your adventure trip fresh.

Credits

Index

Underscored references indicate boxed text.

A

Abdominal muscles
    4-week program summary, 120
    benefits of strong, 119
    cover-model, 16
    crunches, overdoing, 126
    exercises for
        cable chop, 94–95
        double-resistance double crunch, 124
        figure-four double crunch, 84
        hanging reverse trunk twist, 123
        plank, 126
        reverse pushup, 127
        single-resistance double crunch, 123
        stability-ball curlup, 120
        stability-ball curlup with knee tuck, 122
        Swiss-ball knee tuck, 94
        twisting medicine-ball toss, 121
        v raise, 122
        v raise/knee tuck, 124
        v twist, 95
    during weight lifting, 68
    working upper, 76
Acetic acid, blood glucose and, 15–16
Achilles tendinitis, exercises for
    inverted calf raise, 183
    soleus stretch, 183
Active release techniques (ART), 77
Acupressure, for joint pain, 150
Acupuncture, for weight loss, 4
ADD, exercise and, 138
Adenosine triphosphate (ATP), 80
Adrenaline, workouts and, 86
Adventure racing
    conditioning for, 152–54
    core body and, 151–52
    tips for, 153
    women and, 149–50
Adventure sports, training for, 217
Aerobic exercise. *See also* Running
    cognitive function and, 132–35
    duration and intensity, 137

    job performance and, 135–38
    to lose belly fat, 41
    for stress relief, 12
    ways to make time for, 134
Afterburn effect, 39, 41
Agility
    core body development and, 91
    exercises for, 158
    footwork drill for, 170
Air travel, healthy eating and, 10
Alcoholic drinks, at cocktail parties, 11
All Sport drinks, 28
Almonds, for weight loss, 4
Altitude, adjustment to, 161, 180
Alzheimer's disease, salmon and, 20
Ankles
    exercise to strengthen, 175
    kinematic MRIs for, 178
    sprains, exercises to prevent
        balance reach, 184
        peroneal stretch, 184
    tape for, vs. braces, 172
    training on unstable surfaces, 168
Antioxidants
    black tea, 167
    green tea extract, 169
    vitamin C, 166–67
Anxiety, exercise for, 138
Apollo Health goLite P1 lamp, 4
Appetite
    blood glucose and, 15
    lack of sleep and, 28
    suppression, with
        acupuncture, 4
        fish, 25–26
        tomato juice, 10
Arms
    4-week program summary, 105
    benefits of strong, 104
    exercises for
        alternating-grip hammer curl, 106
        bench dip, 82–83